ONE WEEK LOAN

why the constitution matters

yale

university

press

new haven

and

london

mark

tushnet

why

the

constitution

matters

Set in Adobe Garamond type by Keystone Typesetting, Inc., Orwigsburg, Pennsylvania. Printed in the United States of America.

Library of Congress Cataloging-in-Publication Data
Tushnet, Mark V., 1945–
Why the Constitution matters / Mark Tushnet.
    p. cm. — (Why X matters)
Includes bibliographical references and index.
ISBN 978-0-300-15036-0 (hardcover : alk. paper)
1. Constitutional law—United States. 2. Political questions and judicial power—United States. 3. United States. Supreme Court. I. Title.
KF4550.T873   2010
342.7302—dc22   2009049293

A catalogue record for this book is available from the British Library.

This paper meets the requirements of ANSI/NISO Z39.48-1992 (Permanence of Paper).

10 9 8 7 6 5 4 3 2 1

also by mark tushnet

Tushnet, Mark, *The Constitution of the United States of America: A Contextual Analysis* (Hart Publishing, 2009).

Tushnet, Mark, *Weak Courts, Strong Rights: Judicial Review and Social Welfare Rights in Comparative Constitutional Law* (Princeton University Press, 2008).

Tushnet, Mark, ed., *I Dissent: Great Opposing Opinions in Landmark Supreme Court Cases* (Beacon Books, 2008).

Amar, Vikram, and Mark Tushnet, *Global Perspectives on Constitutional Law* (Oxford University Press, 2008).

Fink, Howard, Linda Mullenix, Thomas Rowe, and Mark Tushnet, *Federal Courts in the Twenty-First Century* (LexisNexis 3d ed., 2007).

contents

Introduction   1

one   How the Constitution Matters   19

two   How the Supreme Court Matters   93

three   How to Make the Constitution Matter More—or

Differently   151

Sources   175

Acknowledgments   181

Index   183

why the constitution matters

introduction

Why does the Constitution matter? If you've picked up this book, you probably already have an answer to this question. The Constitution matters, you're likely to think, because it protects our fundamental rights. The answer I provide here is different: The Constitution matters because it provides a structure for our politics. It's politics, not "the Constitution," that is the ultimate—and sometimes the proximate—source for whatever protection we have for our fundamental rights.

Here's a quick introduction to the reasons why your first answer, about fundamental rights, isn't quite right.

People disagree about what our fundamental rights are, and no one really believes that whatever the Supreme Court says those rights are is the last word. Some people think that the Constitution guarantees a pregnant woman a right to choose to have an abortion; others don't, and some even think that the fetus has a constitutionally based right to life enforceable against the woman. Some people think that the Second Amendment protects our right as individuals to own guns for self-protection; others think that this is both a silly interpretation of this amendment, which explicitly refers to a "well-regulated Militia," and a socially disastrous policy in some of our nation's cities. In light of these differences, saying that the Constitution matters because it protects our fundamental rights doesn't tell us anything.

It doesn't help to say, "Well, maybe the Constitution—the words written in the little pamphlets we can get from our members of Congress—doesn't protect our fundamental rights, but the Supreme Court does when it interprets the Constitution." After all, the Supreme Court has said that a woman has a constitutional right to choose an abortion and that the Second Amendment protects our right to own handguns. That's how the Constitution protects our fundamental rights—through constitutional interpretation by the Supreme Court.

In general, though, Supreme Court decisions don't eliminate the disagreements we have about what our fundamental rights are. I have to be careful here. Sometimes the mere fact that the Supreme Court has interpreted the Constitution one way or another does affect what some people think the Constitution means. People more or less in the middle of the political spectrum, who don't care too much about the constitutional provision the Court has interpreted, might say to themselves, "What do I really know about the Constitution? I have mostly uninformed predispositions or prejudices about what it means. But if the Supreme Court says that's what the Constitution means, it must be right. After all, the Justices know a lot more about the Constitution than I do." But, for the most contentious issues the Court addresses—I've been using abortion and the Second Amendment as my examples, but of course there are many others—a lot of people care a lot and have firmly held views about what our fundamental rights are. Their views aren't going to be displaced simply by a Supreme Court decision, or even by a series of decisions on the same question. Indeed, some of them will see the Court's decisions as a reason to try to change the Court's membership by electing a different kind of president who will nominate different kinds of justices. In other words, they will use politics to try to change the Supreme Court and, through the Court, the prevailing interpretation of the Constitution and, through those changes, the content of the fundamental rights Americans actually have. As Chapter Two explains, the "fundamental rights" answer to our question about why the Constitution matters makes sense only after we understand how politics affects the Supreme Court.

Of course, you might be happy right now because the

Supreme Court has been protecting the fundamental rights you like. But if you know anything about constitutional history, you know that that hasn't always been true. It's not as though the Supreme Court has finally reached "enlightenment" and will never change its mind. Someday, maybe soon, the Court is going to start protecting rights you don't think should be protected and stop protecting the ones you like. If you think that the issues you care about most today will become much less important in a few years, you won't care. You'll take what you have now and go home happy. Then, though, you should acknowledge that it's not the Constitution that matters, or even the Supreme Court, but this particular Supreme Court.

What the Supreme Court says our rights are depends in a complicated way on the state of our politics. No one thinks that the Supreme Court justices read the morning papers or political blogs to figure out what the state of our politics is, and therefore how they should interpret the Constitution. (Indeed, some of them have said, credibly, that they don't read newspapers at all.) Still, they are part of our political system. They get to the Court because a president thinks that putting this person rather than that one on the Court will promote some of the president's short- and long-term political interests. Abraham Lincoln reportedly said, "We cannot ask a man what he will do, and if we should, and he should answer us, we would despise him. Therefore we must take a man whose opinions are known." Sometimes the political interests really are short-term, as when Franklin Roosevelt named justices to the Court whom he confidently believed would vote to uphold his New Deal programs. Sometimes the political interests are longer-term, as when Ronald Reagan sought to name justices who would develop and articulate over their careers a constitutional vision that would continue to affect national policy long after Reagan had left the presidency. Senators vote for or against a nominee on similar political grounds.

As these examples indicate, the president is a crucial player in determining what view of fundamental rights the Supreme Court will take. Most of the time presidents take the Court as they find it, because other things are more important to them—for Bill Clinton, for example, the national economy and health care policy. Transforming the Supreme Court would take too much of their political capital, particularly if they don't strenuously object to any of the Court's recent rulings. Occasionally, though, a president will make transforming the Court a central project for his administration. The success of such a campaign depends on whether enough seats become open on the Supreme Court during that president's term in office and on events elsewhere in our political system—particularly whether the Senate is reliably in the hands of the president's allies or is sufficiently divided that opposition party senators decide that they should spend *their* political capital on fighting hard against a transformative nomination.

Behind the president and senators, of course, are the American people. Whether and how we participate in politics set the conditions under which our politicians operate, and so set the conditions for the Court to act. Sometimes the justices themselves change their minds because of larger social changes. This is rare, I think, but almost certainly accounts for the Court's changing views about the constitutional status of women and gays and lesbians. No president has appointed anyone to the Court because of his or her views about those issues, and some justices were almost certainly indifferent to the constitutional arguments asserted on behalf of women and gays and lesbians at the time they were appointed.[1] But, as society changed, in part because of political mobilizations by and on behalf of those communities, so did the views of some justices.

Here, too, politics structures the Supreme Court, and that's how the Constitution matters for our fundamental rights.

Some of the things many of us think are fundamental in our national policies result from legislation, not from Supreme Court interpretations of the Bill of Rights. Recently legal scholars have

---

1. Justice Ruth Bader Ginsburg was appointed in part because of her history as a women's rights lawyer, but by the time of her appointment most—though not all—of the constitutional transformation of women's rights had occurred.

paid attention to what can be called "The Constitution Outside the Constitution." Perhaps we should reserve the capitalized term for the written words in the document displayed in the National Archives. The idea of a constitution outside the Constitution, though, seems essential to understanding our constitutional system. Consider Social Security. Repealing the basic Social Security Act would almost certainly be more difficult than amending the Constitution. Put another way, the Social Security Act is as deeply embedded in our political order as anything in the written Constitution. For that reason, and because of its social importance, the Act should be regarded as "constitutional."

Determining what's in the constitution outside the Constitution calls for careful judgment, and the list should be reasonably short. And there are complexities in working out exactly what it means to put something on that list. For one thing, it can't mean that Congress is unable to change the terms of a statute that's part of the constitution outside the Constitution. It surely can amend the details of the Social Security Act, for example, and has done so, not always to extend its coverage. We need to have some concept of permissible tinkering that we can use to distinguish from large-scale near-repeal. And it can't mean that a court could justifiably strike down a statute because it was somehow inconsistent with the Social Security Act. However we develop the idea, though, we're going to have some statutory schemes on the list. My candidates include the general social safety net of the modern social welfare state, the basic structure of modern environmental law, and the core provisions of our civil rights statutes.

My next point should be obvious, but let me be explicit: The constitution outside the Constitution consists of *statutes* enacted by Congress. These statutes result from our politics. So, once again, the Constitution matters because it provides the structure through which we act politically to get our representatives to enact statutes that will become part of the constitution outside the Constitution.

Beyond all this are really important things about the way we organize ourselves as a society and politically that we take for granted but can't easily tie to the written Constitution. We don't expect a president acting as commander in chief to order military forces into action to suppress his political opponents, for example, and at the same time we expect military officers to do what their civilian chiefs tell them to do. We can struggle to locate these taken-for-granted propositions in the written Constitution—we can see some parts of the idea of civilian control of the military in the provision barring members of Congress from holding positions in the executive branch, for example—but what we can find doesn't seem to correspond well to the assumptions' importance in our overall constitutional system.

Another implication: The written Constitution doesn't even provide the framework within which we argue about what rights are fundamental. "Where in the National Archives do you see that right mentioned?" isn't a good argument against a claim that some right is fundamental, and not merely because the Supreme Court has (controversially) recognized "unenumerated" rights, that is, rights that aren't listed in the pamphlet. It's not a good argument because some of our fundamental rights result from Congress's adoption of important—fundamental—statutes.

Most of the things most Americans think are our most important policies are directly the result of political choices, and the Supreme Court has almost nothing to say about them. Just before the 2008 elections, the American people were worried about the economy, health care, the wars in Iraq and Afghanistan, education, and taxes. In 2009 the list was almost identical, with immigration considered to be a bit more important than it had been a few months earlier. What does the Constitution have to do with these issues? The question is important if we are to understand why—and, more important, how—the Constitution matters.

If we think that the Constitution matters only in Supreme Court cases, we're not going to think that the Constitution matters much to the issues we worry about most. That may be one reason that, despite the best efforts of some advocacy groups, no candidate for the presidency in modern times has been able to get the public to care much about whom he or his rival will appoint to the Supreme Court. Maybe some steps the Obama administration has taken to deal with the economy, or some components of the health care plan it develops, will raise constitutional questions that will get to the Supreme Court. But whatever those questions might be—and there might not be any at all—they will deal with no more than matters on the periphery of the administration's programs. Even the Supreme Court's decisions dealing with the rights of people detained at Guantánamo Bay have only the most modest connection to the nation's efforts to combat terrorism: Deployment of armed forces overseas, clandestine operations, and investigations of noncitizens abroad are surely more important to those efforts' success than whether a handful of detainees receive hearings about their status in which the admissibility of hearsay evidence is limited—the issue that was at stake in the most important of the Supreme Court's decisions.

I think a pause is appropriate here. I began this introduction by saying why the "fundamental rights" answer to the question "Why does the Constitution matter?" wasn't quite right. Much of what I've written to this point, and much of Chapter One, aims at debunking the claim that the Constitution matters because it protects our fundamental rights. But the debunking shouldn't be taken too far. The qualifier *quite* is important. Most of the examples in the introduction acknowledge that the "fundamental rights" answer has something to it, just not enough to provide a full explanation for the Constitution's importance. When you put all the acknowledgments together, what you get is something like this: The Constitution matters because it symbolizes our political culture's commitment to the very idea that we have fundamental rights. That doesn't tell us anything about what those fundamental rights are or how they are protected, but it does tell us that protecting fundamental rights is important to us.

What we need to know is why and how the Constitution matters on the issues that matter most to us, including but not limited to the protection of our fundamental rights whatever they are. We know why elections matter—they put in office the politicians who will make the policies that matter most to us. If the Constitution matters, it does so because it has something to do with politics and elections.

What might that be? We have to begin by taking a step or two back. Obviously, politics in the United States is partisan politics, conducted by the two major political parties with occasional interventions by social movements organized in "civil society," outside the party structure. Notably, though, the Constitution says nothing explicit about political parties. As we will see in Chapter One, the Constitution's framers thought that nationally organized political parties were likely to pernicious influence on public policy and did what they could —not enough, it turned out—to prevent the development of such parties. More recently the Supreme Court has interpreted the Constitution's protection of freedom of expression and assembly to place some limits on the ability of legislatures to prescribe rules by which political parties are organized on the state and national levels. But, again, these interventions have been relatively modest, although one, as we will see, has some implications for recent efforts to tamp down party polarization that might not reflect less polarized opinions within the public at large. Here, too, debunking claims about the importance of the Supreme Court's decisions is valuable, but something remains even after the debunking is done.

So: The issues we care about are decided by politics, not by the Constitution; politics is conducted by political parties that are themselves not recognized in the Constitution. How could the Constitution matter? Basically, because it creates the structure within which our parties operate. The United States has a system in which the president and members of Congress are elected separately, in contrast to parliamentary systems in which the prime minister is chosen by elected party officials. It has a federal system in which political parties are organized on the state level, and state political parties join forces for presidential political campaigns, after which they revert to their local focus. In short, the Constitution matters because political parties matter, and the Constitution has some influence on the way parties operate.

Only some influence, though. Political party organization has changed recently: presidents have been more effective recently in sustaining a national-level political party that provides guidance to party members in Congress—more effective, but not completely so. The national-level parties have become more ideologically coherent, organized less as coalitions of local parties with varying interests and ideological concerns and more as parties with programs to which every member at every level—local, state, House of Representatives, and Senate— is committed. This has occurred, in turn, in part because of greater attention by national party leaders to recruiting candidates for congressional and Senate races. These changes result from political decisions by politicians, about which the Constitution has little to say.[2]

Here's a brief example of how—and how little—the Constitution affects politics and therefore how it affects the policies that matter most to most of us. After the 2008 elections, the conventional wisdom in Washington was that important policy

2. Except in court interpretations that have allowed national politicians to expand national power. Here too the story is primarily about politicians' decisions backed up in the end by the courts.

initiatives could not be adopted unless they had the support of sixty senators, and that obtaining such support was going to be quite difficult. The reason for the sixty-senator requirement was the Senate's filibuster rule that allows debate on any matter —with one important exception—to continue without a time limit, unless sixty senators vote to limit debate. And the reason for the difficulty in cutting off debate was the increasing ideological coherence within the Republican minority, exemplified by the decision of Pennsylvania Senator Arlen Specter to switch from the Republican Party to the Democratic Party.

The filibuster rule has some connection to the Constitution, albeit a tenuous one. The Senate's rules allow unlimited debate, except on the final enactment of the national budget— which allows some policy initiatives to be bundled as part of this "reconciliation" resolution without requiring sixty votes. In contrast the House of Representatives tightly controls debate according to "rules" prescribed by the House Rules Committee.[3] The Constitution "accounts for" this difference, because it gives each house the power to make its own rules.[4]

---

3. That power, again arising from the constitutional power of the House to set its own rules, can and historically did allow the Rules Committee to block House consideration of legislative proposals, mostly liberal ones in the 1950s.

4. It's quite difficult to imagine a workable system in which we had two houses of the legislature and a separately elected president, *and*

As long as the parties were ideologically diverse, the filibuster rule alone wouldn't matter across the board (and it didn't for a long time except for civil rights legislation). Liberal northern Democrats could count on the support of some northeastern Republican allies on some issues, but those Republicans would join their conservative western Republican members on other issues, and similarly with conservative southern Democrats and conservative Republicans. The effect was to make each side leery of threatening a filibuster, for fear of alienating members of the other party who might be needed on some issues (except on the specific issue of civil rights, where segregationist southern senators could count on at most lukewarm support for civil rights among many Republican senators). These fears diminished as the parties became ideologically coherent. To overstate it a bit: No Republican senator is going to vote for a Democratic initiative anyway, so why worry about annoying the Democrats by filibustering everything? Discovering the Constitution's role in promoting partisan ideological coherence is difficult, as we will see. Its main contribution may be a surprising one:

---

rules for the legislative houses set by some other mechanism. The prospect of paralysis if one house's rules had to be approved by the other house, or if both houses' rules had to be signed into law by the president, is evident. There are statutes that do set internal rules, but it's not clear how important they are, or even whether the provisions would be followed in cases where it might matter.

Developments in society and in the economy have encouraged the flow of policy-making power to the national government. Those developments have been facilitated by the Constitution and allowed by the Supreme Court. As the national government has become increasingly important in policy-making, political parties and especially presidents have found it politically advantageous to develop coherent party platforms to which every officeholder is committed.

Much in the preceding paragraphs sounds more like political science than it does constitutional law. The reason is that the most important aspects of constitutional law deal with politics —not, as some politicians like to say in criticizing the Supreme Court, because Supreme Court justices simply enact their policy preferences into constitutional law, but because the Constitution provides the framework for our politics. This book shows how. Chapter One examines the ways in which the Constitution provides the structure for our party system, its relation to modern developments in party organization, and the relatively minor ways in which constitutional doctrine influences that organization. Chapter Two examines the Supreme Court, focusing on *its* relation to political parties—the ways in which politicians find judicial review useful and the ways in which the Supreme Court is affected by social movements that themselves affect political parties.

At the outset I must emphasize that almost everything I say

here is the conventional wisdom among scholars—even legal scholars—who study the Constitution even though the academic lawyers among us don't teach much of what I write about in this book in law school courses in constitutional law. It might look as if we think that the "fundamental rights" answer to the question is the right one, but that's because people usually ask us about the Constitution in connection with some current controversy or a case the Supreme Court has just decided. Such an impression about what constitutional scholars think is important is misleading. The constitutional provisions that help define our politics, the provisions that matter, can be changed only under quite special circumstances—never in litigation, and only once every generation or two through politics itself.

The real question, then, is not *why* the Constitution matters, but *how* it matters. The Constitution matters because politics matters. The Constitution affects politics in many ways, most of those indirect, but we shouldn't overestimate how much it matters.

1

how the constitution matters

The Constitution and National Politics

What does it take for you to get the national health care policy you want? The first thing that's going to come to mind is that you have to get Congress to enact the policy and the president to sign the bill.[1] After that happens, of

1. Actually, it's (barely) imaginable that you could get the Supreme Court to declare that you have a constitutional right to the health care policy you want. The Constitution would *really* matter, a lot, if that was a realistic possibility, but it isn't—which is another way of saying that the Constitution matters less than you might think it does.

course, the Supreme Court has to uphold the statute. When it does—and, on the whole, it will—the Court has to make two decisions. It has to say that the statute lies within the powers granted to the national government by the Constitution, and it has to say that the statute doesn't violate any rights protected by the Constitution. For reasons that we'll examine later, the odds are quite slim that the twenty-first century Supreme Court would find that health care policy lies outside the national government's constitutional power. And, though it might strike down some statutory details because they violated constitutional rights, the chances are high that those details won't have much to do with the basics of the policy Congress and the president approved.[2]

If important policies—the ones that surveys indicate the public cares most about—have to be enacted by Congress, why does the Constitution matter? Of course the Constitution *creates* Congress and the presidency. It requires that we have elections for the House and the Senate, although not for the presi-

---

2. One important qualification: Something that looks like a detail might be more like a linchpin, a feature that is essential to the statute's effective operation even though a nonspecialist—like a judge—might not understand its importance. Invalidating such a provision might be quite important, and a really sophisticated judge who wanted to *effectively* invalidate the statute might do so by latching on to one of these linchpin details.

dency.[3] And, importantly, the president is elected separately from senators and members of the House of Representatives. Senators and representatives are elected from states and districts within states, whereas the president is elected in a national election. A policy favored by a majority in the Senate might not get the agreement of the House, or of the president, because each one's constituencies differ. Indeed, the Senate's rules on "extended debate"—filibusters—mean that a proposal that has majority support in the Senate might not get through that body. The Constitution gives small states more voting power in the Senate than their population (or anything else, as far as anyone can tell) warrants, by guaranteeing that each state, no matter how small or large, has two senators. And if the president disagrees with the House and the Senate, he—someday she—can prevent the proposal from becoming law by vetoing it. Congress can override a president's veto only by getting two-thirds of the members of each house to agree to do so.

3. We vote for presidential "electors," who are the ones whose votes actually count. Of course, by tradition the electors now are pledged to vote for specific candidates. That's a tradition, though, not something required by the Constitution. Nor is the so-called unit rule, under which all the votes of a state's electors are cast for the person who wins a plurality of the popular vote in the state. The "unit rule" is imposed by state law (and Nebraska and Maine don't use it), not by the Constitution.

In creating these institutions, the Constitution obviously matters. If we had a parliamentary system in which the president could stay in office only with the support of a majority in Congress, we *might* get different political outcomes.[4] The "hard-wired" features of our constitutional system are so obvious that nobody really thinks much about them when we ask why the Constitution matters. You read about them in books by political journalists and political scientists, not in columns by journalists who write about the legal system and not in books by people who teach constitutional "law." And perhaps properly so. Describing the features as hard-wired means that they are extraordinarily resistant to alteration. Most of them could be changed only by amending the Constitution—and one, the Constitution's provision that every state—no matter how small—must have the same number of Senators as every other state—no matter how large—can't be amended at all.[5]

4. Not necessarily: Maybe the underlying policy preferences we have would manage to get expressed through the politics associated with a parliamentary system, running through different paths and overcoming different obstacles. Still, it's reasonable to assume that political structures have *some* effects on policy outcomes.

5. There's a peculiar controversy among constitutional scholars about whether this provision actually does protect equal representation in the Senate from amendment. Could we amend the Constitution to eliminate this provision, and then amend the Constitution to apportion the Senate by population? If so, why not do it in one step?

Why spend time worrying about constitutional features that we're almost certainly not going to do anything about?

Another reason for putting hard-wired features to one side is that they might actually be less important than they seem. The filibuster rule is a Senate rule, and the Senate could change the rule if enough Senators wanted to; the rule's not embedded in the Constitution. And today saying that a state is small doesn't tell us much about how its senators are going to vote on basically anything. For Republican Wyoming, there's Democratic Rhode Island. And finally, notice that George W. Bush vetoed only one bill presented to him between 2001 and early 2007.[6] The president's veto power might shape legislation as members of Congress adjust their policy proposals to ensure that the president will sign the bill when it reaches his desk. But, more important, the president doesn't have to veto legislation if his

---

And if in one step, why not simply apportion the Senate by population, on the theory that doing so makes sense only on the assumption that we wanted to change the provision protecting equal representation against amendment? All this is highly theoretical, of course, because there's no chance of any such amendment—and were one to occur, we should probably characterize the events as a minor revolution rather than as a lawful amendment accomplished within the existing constitutional framework.

6. The bill would have provided federal support for stem cell research. Congress failed to override the veto.

party has firm control of one house in Congress.[7] What matters in the first instance are political parties. The Constitution matters to the extent that it affects the party structure in Congress and the presidency.

For a few years toward the beginning of this century we had what political scientists call unified party government. The Republican Party controlled the presidency and both houses of Congress, and that party was quite united ideologically. During that period our separation-of-powers constitutional system operated pretty much the way a parliamentary system would. What makes our constitutional system different from a parliamentary one is the possibility of *divided* government, which can come in various forms. The most obvious is the one we experienced during most of Bill Clinton's presidency—a president from one party, and both houses of Congress controlled by the other party. The popular image is that divided government produces gridlock. Political scientists have shown that the results of divided government are more complicated, because our political parties have been coalitions whose components have had varying ideologies. In the middle of the twentieth century the Democratic Party was a coalition of northern urban liberals

7. Even if the president's party doesn't control Congress, he has a variety of what we'll end up calling "workarounds" to get his way: signing statements, for example, in which the president declares that he will interpret the statute as he chooses, thank you very much.

and southerners who were conservative on racial and social issues but relatively liberal on economic ones, and the Republican Party was a coalition of business-oriented internationalists who were fiscally conservative and relatively liberal on racial and social issues—northeastern or Rockefeller Republicans—and Midwestern isolationists who were more conservative across the board. Even today there are "Blue Dog" Democrats whose version of fiscal conservatism sometimes conflicts with the policies of the rest of the congressional party.

It's worth pausing here to note that I've introduced another structural feature of our constitutional system—federalism. We don't need a technical definition of federalism to understand that our political life has historically been organized around the fact that state and local governments do a lot of the things we care most about. They provide education—influenced by national policies like the so-called No Child Left Behind Act. They provide police protection—with financial assistance from the national government and within boundaries set by the Supreme Court. They pave our streets and build our bridges—again with federal financial assistance. State and local governments *matter* to us, and because they do politicians have historically organized our political parties at the local and state levels—the classic "machines" we've read about in Chicago, New York, and elsewhere. Developments in our national government have reduced the role state political parties play in our political system, but they will almost certainly continue to be important in structuring our politics, if only because the Constitution says that senators will be elected from states, and representatives from districts within states. State and local political parties are where young politicians get trained and bring themselves to the attention of party leaders looking for "good" candidates to run for higher office.

State-based political parties can produce unified or divided government. Divided government doesn't have to produce gridlock when one or both parties are ideological coalitions. Talented party leaders, especially a talented president, can devise significant policies that appeal across party lines to some members of the nominal opposition, and that don't divide the president's party too substantially. The most recent example of an important policy adopted during a period of divided government is the No Child Left Behind statute. Another means of adopting policies during divided government is pure presidential initiative. Dubbed "presidential administration" by Elana Kagan, the practice involves policies chosen by the president that he couldn't get Congress to enact but that stick because the opposition in Congress isn't strong enough to block them. According to Kagan, President Bill Clinton pioneered in the aggressive use of presidential administration, but George W. Bush may have pushed the envelope even further with initiatives on detention of prisoners taken in the "war on terror" and on surveillance of telephone and e-mail communications. Notably, the courts haven't intervened effectively to derail these initiatives. Even when the courts invalidated Bush administration policies, they didn't actually order effective remedies, allowing the administration to leave the problems for its successor to handle.[8]

Notice how my argument has developed. Starting with the observation that the Constitution created a separation-of-powers system, I've argued that separation of powers in itself isn't the driving force behind the policies the American people care about. Rather, what matters is whether government is unified or divided, which depends on political parties, and whether the political parties are ideologically unified or ideological coalitions. Further, the way our political parties are organized is connected to the fact that we have a federal system in which state and local governments make many of the policies people think most important to them.

But no matter how hard you look, you're not going to find

8. During the Bush administration not a single detainee was released from custody pursuant to an order directing that release, although some individual detainees were released after plea bargains or other negotiated deals reached when courts said that something had to be done about them.

anything about political parties in the Constitution, much less anything about internal party structures.[9] The reason lies in our constitutional history. The Constitution's framers knew about political parties, which they called "factions," and they didn't like them. They thought that parties were necessarily going to be devoted to narrow interests—for them, probably important local economic interests—rather than to the interest of the nation as a whole. They did what they could to obstruct the development of political parties organized on a national scale. Look at the original provision for the president's election. Voters cast their votes for electors, as we still do. Those electors were then to meet separately in their home states and vote for two candidates, without distinguishing between candidates for the presidency and the vice presidency. The framers expected that electors would chose favorite-son candidates, or at least regional favorites, and that most of the time no single candidate would have a majority of the electoral votes. If so, the House of Representatives, with each state delegation casting a single vote, would choose the president from the top *five* candi-

9. More modern constitutions than ours do deal with political parties and sometimes with their internal structures. Some constitutions, for example, require that a legislator who leaves her political party give up her seat. Compare the U.S. practice, in which Arlen Specter could change party affiliations with no immediate adverse consequences.

dates. It's the number "five" here that's probably the most revealing: The framers assumed that there would often be five plausible candidates for the presidency, because they assumed that "factions" would form on a local or regional basis but not on a national one.

They were wrong, of course. Within a decade differences between Thomas Jefferson and John Adams produced coordinated actions by political leaders throughout the United States that were the political parties the very same men had feared when writing the Constitution. The 1800 elections showed how badly the original Constitution was designed for a world with political parties. Jeffersonian Democrats ran a ticket throughout the country with Jefferson as the presidential candidate and Aaron Burr as the candidate for vice president. The Jeffersonians won, but they didn't coordinate their actions in the electoral college well enough. Remember, the members of the electoral college actually cast their votes in separate state meetings, and in 1800 communicating with the members wasn't a matter of sending an e-mail to them. After the electoral college returns came in, Jefferson and Burr had exactly the same number of votes. That threw the election into the House of Representatives, where the Federalist candidates John Adams and Charles Cotesworth Pinckney were also on the ballot. Burr refused to withdraw from contention, and the House faced a major political crisis. Eight states had Jeffersonian majorities in their delegations, six had Federalist majorities, and two were evenly divided. The result: no majority for Jefferson because eight isn't a majority of sixteen. After a week of backroom maneuvering, the Federalists in the two divided states chose to be statesmen and voted for Jefferson, allowing him to take office.

The framers were wrong in thinking that they had designed a Constitution that would place real obstacles in the way of the development of national political parties. They were wrong too to think that national political parties were necessarily going to be "factions," organized around specific and relatively clear political platforms that parties once in power would implement. The national political parties have always had political platforms, of course. But the relation between their platforms and what their leaders do once elected has been fairly loose. Here separation of powers and federalism have mattered. Presidential candidates can run on a party's platforms, but to govern after being elected they have to get senators and representatives to go along. Because members of Congress are elected separately from the president, they sometimes—and historically, often—are not seriously committed to all parts of the national party's platform.[10] Here the reason is that the planks in the national

10. The contrast with Great Britain is instructive. There the parties issue election "manifestoes," which are serious outlines for the legisla-

parties' platforms have not always been ideologically consistent. For Democrats, for example, some planks have appealed to urban liberals while others have appealed to southern farm interests. The party "unites" around the platform because everyone figures that getting a Democratic president is better than getting a Republican one, but everyone also knows that fights over whether to enact platform planks will persist after the election.

Over the course of the late twentieth century the two major national political parties became increasingly coherent ideologically—and polarized, to the point where, according to some measures, the most conservative elected Democrat is sometimes more liberal than the most liberal elected Republican. Sometimes commentators explain party polarization as a result of replacing candidate selection by party "bosses" with candidate selection in party primaries, because voters in party primaries tend to be those most committed to ideological positions that distinguish their party from the other. Election by districts also affects party polarization because legislatures can draw district lines to make one party dominant in the districts, with the

---

tion the winning party will introduce. It is a matter of serious "constitutional" concern in Great Britain that a party leader fails to pursue something included in the election manifesto.

effect of making the party primary the election that determines who goes to Congress. There's pretty clearly something to that scenario, but it can't be the whole story, because polarization characterizes the Senate as well as the House of Representatives, and district lines can't affect senatorial elections.

The Constitution's been amended since 1800, but none of the amendments say anything about political parties.[11] If political parties as coalitions or as ideologically unified and polarized drive the adoption of the policies we care most about, does the Constitution really matter? Maybe so, if there's some connection between the Constitution and political parties even though they aren't mentioned.

And there are such connections. Three are especially important: federalism, the presidency, and the First Amendment as interpreted by the Supreme Court. Federalism matters because political parties have historically been organized on the local and state levels, coming together only to elect a president who helped dole out benefits to his supporters in the states and cities. Interacting in a complex way with this feature of our politics is the flow of power to the national government over

11. The Twelfth Amendment, adopted in 1804, fixed the particular problem Burr created, by requiring electors to vote separately for a presidential and a vice presidential candidate. It also reduced the number of candidates from whom the House had to chose, from five to three.

the course of the twentieth century. Increasing national power makes party control of the national government more important than it used to be, and so increases the importance of nationally organized parties. Changes in the technology of politics, especially fund-raising by national organizations supporting presidential candidates, reduced the importance of state-based political parties, but they still have some effects on the strength of each party's ideological coherence. The presidency matters because presidents (and presidential candidates) can articulate unifying ideologies more effectively than any other political leaders can, and they can formulate and attempt to push through Congress political programs that give political parties enduring identities. The First Amendment as interpreted by the Supreme Court matters—somewhat—because it limits the ability of governments to affect a party's internal organization, including its efforts to achieve ideological coherence or to tolerate divisions within a coalitional party, and to regulate how we finance elections.

Federalism and National Party Politics

Federalism matters because it's the best explanation for why we have a two-party system—though not because the Constitution says much about state and local elections or even about congressional elections. The list of constitutional provisions expressly dealing with those elections is short indeed.[12]

- The "Guarantee" Clause says, "The United States shall guarantee to every State in this Union a Republican Form of Government." The Clause's precise meaning is unclear, and the Supreme Court in 1848 said that it wasn't going to interpret the clause, a decision that it has assiduously followed ever since. We know that it means that states can't make their governing positions hereditary, and it almost certainly means that states have to have popular elections to select enough officials to ensure popular control over the government. But a state can have an elected governor and an appointed attorney general, or an elected legislature and an appointed state board of education. And the possibilities for eliminating elections on the local level are almost endless.
- Several constitutional amendments say that *if* you have elections, you can't exclude people from voting on various grounds such as race or gender or failure to pay a fee

12. As we'll see, the First Amendment's guarantee of free speech and association has been interpreted to affect the way states can regulate political parties. And with some creativity we can add a few more provisions to the list, but the added ones really do have no effect on party structure.

for the privilege of voting (a poll tax), and the Supreme Court has interpreted the Constitution's guarantee of equal protection of the laws to impose somewhat broader restrictions on a state's ability to restrict the franchise when it uses elections. But, again, there's no strong constitutional requirement that state and local positions be filled through elections, and many important positions in many states are not.

- Members of the House of Representatives are to be "chosen every second Year by the People." The Constitution, adopted in 1789, provided that senators, who serve six-year terms, would be chosen by state legislatures. The Seventeenth Amendment, adopted in 1913, replaced that with direct popular elections for the Senate.[13] Both provisions leave it to the states to determine the qualifications of voters, subject to the nondiscrimination requirements just mentioned.
- Senators are sorted into three "classes," and—unless there's been a resignation or death—only one senator is chosen when a state holds an election for senator.
- The Constitution says that the states have the power to choose "the Times, Places and Manner of holding

13. These provisions are accompanied by various technical provisions dealing with how to fill seats made vacant by death or resignation.

Elections for Senators and Representatives," but Congress "may at any time by Law make or alter such Regulations." A state legislature could decide to elect all the state's representatives in a single statewide election, using proportional representation. Congress has stepped in, though, and requires that states use single-member districts.[14]

· The House and the Senate have the power to resolve contested elections for seats in those bodies.

And that's it. What do these provisions have to do with our party system?

A key feature of that system is that political parties don't really have members. You're a Republican or a Democrat if you vote consistently for Republicans or Democrats, nothing more. You don't have to pay dues, show up for party meetings, help design the party's platform, or anything else. Why do we have political parties? Mostly because we have local and state governments that provide lots of things people want. People become political activists at the local level to get schools built or roads repaired. Ambitious politicians capitalize on those policy

14. The Supreme Court has held that these districts have to be drawn so that there is as small a departure from strict mathematical equality as can be achieved. I discuss other sorts of gerrymandering later in this chapter.

preferences to win office so that they can advance the policies *they* like, or because they simply like power and the respect that sometimes goes along with it, or to benefit from what the nineteenth century machine politician George Washington Plunkitt called "honest graft," the financial advantages associated with the ability to award government contracts.

Historically, then, American parties were organized at the local and state levels. Saying that someone was a Democrat didn't really tell you a lot because you had to know whether he was Democrat from Alabama or a Democrat from Pennsylvania, and even then you'd want to know whether he came from Philadelphia or Pittsburgh. Why, then, do we have national political parties? Mostly because the national government can supply things to local politicians. Instead of raising local taxes for a road construction program, politicians can use national tax revenues. For this to happen, though, the local politicians have to be able to control or at least strongly influence the national ones. For a long time in our history that was easy. The original Constitution made this sort of control transparent for senators, who were chosen by state legislatures. Even members of the House of Representatives were groomed for higher office by working with and for local political organizations.

The Constitution doesn't mention political parties, but the provisions I've listed have some effects on how parties are organized. The most important is that single-member districting (which includes senatorial elections) pushes in the direction of having only two parties, especially when it's coupled with the rule that whoever gets the most votes in a district wins even if she hasn't received a majority of the votes.[15] If you're electing ten people at once and the top ten vote-getters win, a candidate might be able to win with only 10–15 percent of the vote unless parties assemble tickets that run together and voters don't split their votes. So you can end up with three, four, or more political parties in these districts. When there's only one position to be filled and all you need to win is to get more votes than anyone else, though, you have a pretty strong incentive to assemble a reasonably broad coalition—appealing to the voters in the middle of the political spectrum. Basically, in single-member districts with winner-takes-all rules only two candidates have a realistic possibility of winning.

Single-member districting with a winner-takes-all rules pushes toward having two parties within each district, but that doesn't explain why we don't see *different* parties in each district. One reason is the statewide district for Senate elections and for gubernatorial elections. The two parties that dominate those elections have resources—money, personnel, lists of sympa-

15. Political scientists call this "Duverger's Law" because it was first explained by the French political scientist Maurice Duverger.

thetic voters—they can supply to candidates for Congress and for lower-level state elections. Probably more important, political parties supply "brand names" to candidates. Think of political parties as motel franchises. When someone runs as a Democrat, voters have a rough sense of where that person stands on the political spectrum, just as you know pretty much what you're going to get when you walk into a Quality Inn rather than a Motel 6. Historically, though, it was only a rough sense, because statewide parties were coalitions of local parties, and what mattered to Democrats in upstate New York might be different from what mattered to Democrats in Brooklyn. The breakfast bar at a Quality Inn in Iowa may be more like the breakfast bar across town at the Motel 6 than like the one at a Quality Inn in Colorado. As we'll see, developments in the late twentieth century led to greater party discipline, thereby improving the information conveyed by the party as brand name.

Note, though, that Quality Inn and Motel 6 are national brand names. There are regional brands, but they tend to have smaller market shares even within their regions. So too with national political parties. Over the course of U.S. history, the national government has accumulated the power to do more things that people care about. People therefore care about who controls the national government more than they used to.

When you vote for a local Republican candidate, you want some assurance that the other Republicans in Congress, and the Republican candidate for the presidency, will want to implement a good chunk of the policies your local candidate says she will work to enact. The more power the national government has, the larger the pressure on parties to adopt a platform shared across regions.

These dynamics affect the creation of national political parties—a structural pressure toward having two parties, organizational advantages provided by brand names—and historically produced major parties that were loose coalitions. And coalitions form and reform shifting majorities even without changes in party labels. As the Senate's majority leader in the 1950s, Lyndon Johnson, himself a southerner, was able to hold southern Democrats in a coalition with more liberal urban ones by his mastery of the legislative process, ensuring that everyone in the coalition got something and that no one lost too much. For much of the 1970s liberal nationally oriented Democrats found themselves stymied by a coalition of conservative southern Democrats and conservative Republicans. We can note one important generalization from this. For much of our history we almost necessarily had *effectively* divided government. No matter what the president's ideological orientation, to succeed he had to cobble together support from senators and representatives from both parties.

The President and National Party Politics

Discussing how the president affects the policies the nation pursues because of his relation to political parties will sound a lot like American Government 101, not Con Law 101. Federalism and a handful of constitutional provisions have something to do with the structure of our party system. Constitutional text matters much less for the presidency and the party system. That's because the connection between the Constitution and the president's role in a policy-making process in which political parties play a major part is quite loose—something we can see by noting, once again, that the president's role in making policy has changed over the course of our history, without any relevant changes in the Constitution's text. Probably the most important constitutional provision here is the Twenty-Second Amendment, limiting a president to two four-year terms. This gives a president a foreseeably limited time period in which to accomplish anything, and helps define the challenges a president who hopes to be a national leader must overcome.

Political scientists have given us a powerful conceptual tool for thinking about the presidency. They describe American political history as a succession of "regimes," by which they mean relatively long-term arrangements that combine programmatic commitments—the development of a social safety net for Franklin Roosevelt and Lyndon Johnson, deregulation for Ronald Reagan—with distinctive institutional arrangements. When things go smoothly for a regime, the programs and the institutions exist in a symbiotic relation, with the institutions providing voters with reasons for supporting the regime's programs. Eventually, though, regimes degenerate. Their programs and especially their institutions develop pathologies. Programs became ideologies resistant to adaptation when the facts on the ground cast doubt on whether it makes sense to push the programs further. Institutions become rigid and self-interested, often corrupt in the usual sense. Talented and ambitious politicians come to the fore to offer the public a new vision of public policy—a new regime, in short: "Change We Can Believe In," for example.

We can see the importance of these regimes by considering the two regimes that dominated the twentieth century.

The New Deal/Great Society regime. Programmatically the New Deal/Great Society regime was committed to the expansion of national power to ensure economic stability, to economic security guaranteed by a social safety net, to substantive equality among all citizens achieved by programs like affirmative action, and to protection of liberties associated with personal autonomy.[16] Institutionally the regime created the

16. The Great Society layered the latter two goals onto the first two, which were the New Deal's.

nation's great bureaucracies, symbolized by the Social Security Administration but encompassing all the agencies of the modern administrative state. The regime's programs created constituencies invested in perpetuating the bureaucracies that delivered the goods—the interest groups that dominated Washington's policy-making in mid-century. The presidents who built this regime thought that these interest groups would help them overcome the coalitional party politics of the congressional Democratic Party. The interest groups would mobilize voters to support the presidents' programs, making an end run around the congressional party.

The New Deal/Great Society regime degenerated, of course. The programmatic commitment to economic security became increasingly expensive, the commitment to substantive equality ran up against a deeply rooted ambivalence among white Americans about racial equality, the commitment to personal liberty became associated with rising crime rates and with practices like abortion and recreational drug use that made many working class supporters of the regime's economic policies quite nervous. The bureaucracies became mindless, big government at its worst. And members of Congress learned how to use interest groups for their own purposes, against the president's initiatives.

The Reagan Revolution. Conservative Republicans replaced the degenerating New Deal/Great Society regime with their own, which achieved a fair amount of programmatic success but achieved less in the way of institution-building before it too degenerated. As Reagan put it in his first inaugural address, "government is not the solution to our problem; government is the problem." Programmatically, the Reagan Revolution was committed to deregulation of the national economy and limiting the government's role in altering the distribution of wealth that resulted from "free markets," formal rather than substantive equality, and government regulation of personal autonomy in the service of public morals. Institutionally, it sought to scale back the bureaucracies built up during the prior regime by supporting various forms of voucher programs that allowed people to use public funds to purchase services in the market rather than receiving the services from the government itself and eventually by outsourcing traditional government functions. It also sought to "defund the left" by dramatically reducing public support for institutions it associated with the political opposition and, again eventually, by making it clear that political lobbyists who associated with the opposition would have a hard time getting heard by conservatives in Congress and in the executive branch.

The Reagan Revolution too degenerated. Social conservatism pushed well beyond the limits of public tolerance when Congress enacted the "Terry Schiavo" law, a statute aimed at ensuring that life support would not be removed from a single individual, for example. Deregulation almost by definition could not produce new institutions to support the regime's programs. Outsourcing held out some interesting political possibilities, but posed a serious risk—which materialized on occasion—of ordinary corruption.

Political scientist Stephen Skowronek provides a framework that helps us understand why the Constitution matters for changes in regimes. Noting that presidents want to achieve something—they don't run for the office just for the heck if it—Skowronek describes presidents in relation to political regimes. For our purposes three presidential types matter. First there are the *reconstructive* presidents like Roosevelt and Reagan. They take office when a regime has degenerated and offer a new vision of public policy. Once a new regime is in place, successors from within the same party are *affiliated* presidents—Truman and George H. W. Bush, for example. They face tricky political problems. They understandably think of themselves as serious policy-makers able to make their own contributions to the nation, yet they are almost inevitably viewed in the shadow of their reconstructive predecessors. They engage in what Skowronek calls a "politics of articulation," tweaking their predecessors' principles to make them their own. If they arrive at the presidency when the regime to which they are committed is degenerating, they are almost certainly doomed to failure. Here the modern example is Jimmy Carter, a president affiliated with the degenerating New Deal/Great Society regime. Finally there are presidents like Eisenhower and Clinton, who take office when a regime is robust but who come from the nominal opposition party. Skowronek calls them *preemptive* presidents. They too face real problems. "Their" party isn't really committed to the principles of the regime in place, but the regime's robustness means that the president can't do much to satisfy his partisan allies. A preemptive president has to figure out some way to appropriate the regime's principles and institutions and turn them—ever so slightly, perhaps—in a different direction. It's a difficult task, and makes a preemptive president vulnerable. Noting that Richard Nixon, a preemptive president who tried to pave the way for a reconstructive one, resigned to avoid impeachment, in 1993 Skowronek made the stunningly accurate prediction that the then newly elected William Clinton faced a similar risk of impeachment.

It's worth observing that impeachment—unquestionably a "constitutional" issue—has come into the discussion by way of an analysis of the structure of the presidency and party politics. We'll see in Chapter Two how regime politics helps explain why it's become natural to think that the Constitution matters because it protects fundamental values. For the moment, we can sketch the connection between regime politics, the Supreme Court, and the Constitution. The institutional initiatives reconstructive presidents undertake are sometimes, perhaps often, vulnerable to constitutional challenges. After all, the reconstructive presidents are repudiating central features of the prior regime, yet the judges in place when the reconstructive president arrives on the scene were probably appointed when the prior regime was robust. The constitutional law they developed almost certainly could be used to undermine reconstructive initiatives. And sometimes that's happened. But, in the end, the important point is this: The Supreme Court eventually lets the president and Congress get away with their innovations. It's hard to say that the Constitution "matters" when successive regimes with quite different commitments get what they want, although of course delay can matter a lot to people who don't get what they need or want quickly enough.

Today we tend to think of a president as the party leader as well as the nation's chief executive. In some sense that's obviously true. The president speaks to and for the American people in a way that no other national political figure can. Party platforms are often just a jumble of proposals designed to satisfy parts of the party coalition without alienating too many outside the party. Most modern presidents try to offer something more—not merely discrete policy proposals but a larger vision that unifies the proposals the president decides to push for. Notably, though, the president's agenda is rarely drawn from the party platform on which he nominally ran—unless, of course, the president dictated the party platform before accepting the nomination.

The president's relation to the political party he leads is hardly straightforward. Our separation-of-powers system means that each major political party has two separate wings. The congressional party is always with us. In modern times the presidential party usually comes into being when a party's candidate wins the presidency, and basically disappears if the presidential candidate loses. Because they are elected from different constituencies, the president and members of Congress within a single party can have quite different views about what policies the nation should pursue. And for much of American history they did.

Reconstructive presidents have a particularly difficult task. They were elected because they offered the American people policies decisively different from those we had been getting from the prior "degenerating" regime. The different election cycles for the presidency and for the Senate—products of the Constitution, of course—mean that just after their election reconstructive presidents typically face a Senate with substantial representation from the opponents they have just defeated. The Senate's rules, though not prescribed by the Constitution, can make it difficult for reconstructive presidents to overcome that opposition. This difficulty is sometimes compounded and sometimes reduced when parties are coalitions. A reconstructive president can face opposition from within his party even in the House of Representatives (all of whose members were elected at the same time as the president) as well as in the Senate. But a talented reconstructive president can lure members of the opposition party into a governing coalition, as Ronald Reagan did with conservative Democrats and as Barack Obama has attempted with moderate Republicans.

Parties as coalitions pose similar problems for all presidents. Once a regime is firmly established, of course, presidents who practice a politics of articulation may have an easier job. Their party will have a substantial majority in Congress, and the opposition party will share the regime's general commitments though it will differ over the details of implementing those commitments. But regimes always degenerate, and ambitious politicians are always on the lookout for opportunities to move up in the world—by accelerating the degeneration or by offering a new reconstructive vision. Here too federalism matters. It gives such politicians a political base independent of the president, particularly in the statewide constituencies of governors and senators.

At the end of the twentieth century new forms of party organization emerged, with important consequences for the way in which our constitutional system operates. The dynamic was simple, the explanations complex. America's political parties began to lose their coalitional characteristics and became more ideologically coherent, more like European parties. The brand name began to mean more.

We can begin by describing the way candidates were chosen in the nineteenth century. The Constitution itself says nothing about how congressional and presidential candidates are to be chosen.[17] For much of the nineteenth century and into the twentieth leading figures within each party—people we now pejoratively describe as "bosses"—were the key players. At first presidential nominations were made by what critics called "King Caucus," consisting of each party's congressional delegation. Those members, of course, were themselves the products of local parties. They met, considered potential candidates, made backroom deals, and came up with someone whom they thought could win the election. Martin Van Buren, who served as President Andrew Jackson's chief political lieutenant before becoming president himself, believed that the caucus system

---

17. That might be a slight overstatement. Constitutional amendments guaranteeing that the right to vote will not be denied on the basis of race and gender, for example, might apply to some mechanisms of candidate selection, notably the presidential primaries, which have become the way candidates are chosen today. Even if they don't apply directly (and they might not, for reasons we'll see later in this chapter), a political party seriously interested in winning elections would be committing suicide if it attempted to exclude voters from primaries on the basis of race or gender.

ran too great a risk of generating many regional candidates. He substituted the party convention, with delegates chosen by local political leaders. On the local level these leaders sometimes held major offices themselves. Often, though, they held minor political positions or none at all, exercising power behind the scenes, perhaps because the talents needed for organizing a political party and getting out the vote were different from those needed by mayors and governors. The delegates these politicians chose, the direct participants in the process, tended to be elected officials themselves—senators, congressmen, governors, and mayors who led local political organizations that among other things could get out the vote for the party's presidential candidate.

Starting early in the twentieth century and culminating in the century's last decades, candidate selection changed in ways that affected each party's ideological coherence. The changes in party structure resulted from law, technology, and creativity in designing new national party institutions.

Law. The Progressive political movement late in the nineteenth century and through the first decades of the twentieth objected to the dominant role they saw political bosses playing. Progressives sought to weaken the bosses' hold with many reforms. The first to succeed, at least in part, was the replacement of patronage appointments to government offices with a competitive civil service system. People who got jobs through patronage would reward their patrons with political support and "honest graft"; people who got their jobs based on merit would simply do the public's work.

Next came reforms in candidate selection. As noted above, the Seventeenth Amendment put the election of senators directly in the people's hands, replacing selection by state legislatures. Almost simultaneously Progressives pushed for the candidate selection through party primaries. For many years the political bosses were able to control the outcomes of primaries because they could get their supporters to the polls (and because many states didn't hold primary elections at all), while insurgents had a harder time. Eventually, though, candidates who for all practical purposes "nominated" themselves gained ground. As the title of one book written by a political scientist in 1990 put it, we now elect "actors, athletes, and astronauts"—a list to which we can now add professional comedians. Sometimes people were able to nominate themselves simply because they were rich enough to spread their name across the district or the state. By the early 1970s, party primaries were virtually the only way presidential candidates were nominated. The "brokered" convention, in which party leaders could guide the convention's outcome, disappeared.

Candidate selection through primaries, in which party leaders played a relatively small role, pushed the parties apart. With the demise of political machines to bring out the vote, and in the absence of real membership-based political parties, the people who vote in party primaries tended to be those most devoted to party positions—Republicans who were more conservative than most voters, Democrats who were more liberal. Self-nominated candidates tended to be interested in specific issues, typically toward the left (for Democrats) or right (for Republicans) of the positions taken by party professionals.[18]

To some extent this effect was exacerbated by changes in the way district lines were drawn, although political scientists argue about precisely how significant the effects are. Starting in the 1960s the Supreme Court insisted that each district in a legislature have almost exactly the same number of voters. The nation had a long history of gerrymandering, that is, drawing district lines to guarantee that the people who were elected had some desirable characteristics, whether in terms of supporting specific policies or because they were good party members. The Court's decisions basically meant that gerrymandering could now be done only to obtain partisan advantage—to design secure Democratic or Republican seats or to maximize the number of seats the dominant party will probably win, a strategy

18. This is probably the best place to observe that the political features I'm describing are tendencies, not universal rules, and that it's relatively easy to find exceptions to the tendencies. Yet, the effects on our party structure result from the general sweep of things, not the exceptional cases.

that can misfire because sometimes it requires the dominant party to shift some of its supporters from districts in which the party has a large majority into one where its numbers are small enough that even with the new voters packed in the party runs a risk of losing the district election. And politicians were hardly averse to doing so. The result: a lot of districts in which the minority party had no chance of being elected, the real election was the party primary, the only voters who mattered were the most partisan, and the winning candidates more to the left or right than the general public. Not surprisingly, partisan polarization in legislatures increased.[19]

Finally, reforms in campaign finance law, discussed below, increased the power within each party of their most active and therefore most ideological members and weakened the role party leaders themselves could play.

Institutional innovation and technology. Reconstructive presidents, we've seen, try to displace existing party organizations. Roosevelt did so by creating administrative bureaucracies. By the turn of the twenty-first century national politicians had figured out ways of using new technologies to strengthen their hand.

19. As I noted earlier, partisan gerrymandering can't be the whole story, though, because polarization has increased in the Senate as well as the House of Representatives, and senators are elected from non-gerrymandered statewide districts.

A simple innovation—the computer—made partisan gerry-mandering easier. The U.S. census provided the basic data, which by the twenty-first century gave details about districts down to the level of city blocks. Combine that with the results reported from polling places, and you can get a pretty good grasp of where each party is strong or weak. Then all it takes is a program to put the puzzle's pieces together subject only to the requirement that districts have the same population.

Politicians also discovered what commercial advertisers knew —that direct mail to "consumers" made a difference. Commer-cial mailing lists gave hints about who might be interested in what sorts of messages: subscribers to *Shooting Times* maga-zine were likely to be sympathetic to gun-rights messages from Republican candidates, for example. And not just messages— politicians began to use direct mail to solicit contributions in small amounts from enthusiastic donors. Direct mail served the same purpose as Roosevelt's bureaucracies, connecting vot-ers directly to national-level politicians over the heads of local political leaders. These developments created the possibility of a permanent presidential party, suggested by Barack Obama's effort to sustain his hugely successful Internet-based fund-raising operation by transforming it into a mechanism to sup-port his presidential policy agenda.

The weakening of local political machines opened up space for candidate recruitment by the national political parties and especially by the presidential party. In some tension with the increase in self-nominated candidates, this recruitment nonetheless tended to produce an increasing amount of ideological coherence within each party. Throughout most of U.S. history, presidents played a small role at most in choosing congressional candidates. Franklin Roosevelt famously intervened in southern primary elections in 1938, attempting to replace the conservative Democrats who were causing him problems with New Dealers, and he came a cropper. By the end of the twentieth century both parties were on the lookout for "good" candidates to run. They offered various benefits to the candidates they tapped: media training and "talking points," for example. And, most important of all, financial support. Running a congressional campaign became extremely expensive, and national party organizations helped relieve their favored candidates of the fund-raising burden. Here the effect was to bring the congressional party into line with the presidential one—or, put another way, to convert the party-as-coalition into a more homogeneous party. It's not clear whether these relatively recent changes are permanent, although my view is that they are, and that our thinking about how the Constitution matters for the next decades will have to take them into account.

It's worth emphasizing that all these innovations were not "natural." They required institutional creativity by astute politicians. Those who innovate early gain important advantages.

Eventually, though, pretty much everyone catches on, and the overall party structure changes.

Congress, the presidency, and party structure: these are what matter most to most of us most of the time, because these are what produce the policies that are at the heart of our public life. The Constitution's connection to these features exists, obviously. We *have* a Congress and a presidency because of the Constitution. Beyond that, though, the Constitution's effects are indirect and probably small. The Constitution's provisions might affect a politician's incentives. Members of the House of Representatives run for election every two years, which gives them strong reasons to get things done for their districts quickly. A president sees the end of his term in front of him during his second term and has to figure out what to do to make his mark on history. But we shouldn't exaggerate how much the Constitution matters for these structural issues.

The First Amendment and National Party Politics

Because political parties are associations that engage in political speech, government regulation of political parties brings the First Amendment into play. So, perhaps the Constitution overall isn't that important, but if political parties are important and the First Amendment affects the way our political parties operate, maybe the Constitution matters more, or in a different way, than I've indicated so far. Here too at least some debunking is appropriate. Much of what the Supreme Court has said about political parties and the First Amendment probably doesn't have much effect on how they operate, but some of its decisions —most notably, those dealing with the regulation of campaign finance—might matter. In the end, I'm skeptical even about that claim, but in my view it's more substantial than other claims about why the Constitution matters.

The Supreme Court's cases dealing with the regulation of parties and especially with the regulation of campaign finance are quite complicated, with some aspects giving the First Amendment the feel of the Internal Revenue Code's complexity. Broadly stated, the Court's decisions allow state governments to favor the two major parties if they want to, but prohibit them from completely denying third parties the opportunity to win elections by making it too hard for them to get on the ballot. Perhaps more important, though, the decisions also bar governments from trying to offset party polarization by regulating party primaries with an eye to encouraging the selection of candidates who will appeal more to the general electorate than to party activists.

We have to start with a minor puzzle. Standard First Amendment doctrine is highly suspicious of laws that regulate political expression. So why do state governments have any power to regulate political parties?[20]

- *Historical accident.* States began to regulate political parties in the early twentieth century, by requiring candidate selection in primary elections, before the Supreme Court began to develop its vigorous free speech jurisprudence. When the Court got around to thinking about state regulation of political parties, too much water had passed under the bridge for the Court to intervene too strongly. In a relatively early case involving the First Amendment and political parties, for example, the Court said in 1974 that it was "too plain for argument" that a state could require parties to choose candidates in primary elections to ensure that disagreements within the parties are resolved democratically.
- *Consumer protection.* The states say to candidates, You want us to put your name on the ballot with a party label attached to it. We have to be sure that you really do represent the party you say you do. But parties are really loose associations here—whoever shows up at a party meeting, whoever attends a party convention, whoever

20. It's worth noting that once again we see the role of states—that is, federalism—in structuring our party system.

registers as a party member, whoever votes in a party primary, is a "member." We have to establish some ground rules to make sure that you're really entitled to use the brand name you're claiming.[21]

· *The legacy of segregation.* In decisions starting in the 1930s and ending in the early 1950s the Supreme Court dealt with constitutional questions about "white primaries" in the one-party South. First the Court struck down state laws that restricted participation in Democratic Party primaries to whites—not under the First Amendment, but under the Equal Protection Clause, because the state laws discriminated on the basis of race. After some southern states repealed those laws, the Court said that as long as the states gave parties some special role in the election process, the parties couldn't limit voting in the primary to whites. In the jargon of constitutional law, political parties—at least in the one-party South—were "state actors." In the most expansive ruling, the Court held that this was true even where the

21. Sometimes, though, party meetings aren't as open as they seem. Former congressman and judge Abner Mikva tells the story of his initial foray into Chicago politics: He showed up at the political clubhouse and was asked who sent him. When he said, "Nobody," meaning that he was simply interested in taking part in Chicago politics, the old hands there replied, "We don't want nobody nobody sent."

"primary" was a fairly informal poll conducted by a "club" within the party, when the club's decisions had always been followed by the party itself.[22] The implication of these decisions was that the First Amendment didn't give the major parties the right to select candidates however they wanted.[23] Most states now require those parties to choose candidates for major offices in primary elections or in conventions that are open to any party member. And it seems to be settled that these requirements don't violate the First Amendment.

- *"Neutral" regulations.* Finally, state regulation of political parties fits, a bit uncomfortably, into the Court's First Amendment jurisprudence. Oversimplifying an extremely complicated body of law: With what are misleadingly described as narrow exceptions, governments

22. Language in these cases says that the Constitution restricts party decisions when the party's choice of candidate is effectively the end of the campaign, because the Democratic Party was so dominant in the South in the 1930s and 1940s that whoever the Democrats chose inevitably won the election. I think that most constitutional scholars today are skeptical about the present-day applicability of these cases to elections in districts dominated by a single party because of partisan gerrymandering.

23. Early on, and through more recent decisions, the Court protected minor parties, especially those with truly distinctive political platforms, from these state regulations.

can't regulate speech because of its content unless it has a really strong reason to believe that the speech is going to cause really serious social harm.[24] But, governments can regulate all speech within a general category in what's called a "facially neutral" way, if the regulations are "reasonable" and don't put too large a burden on the speaker.[25] The fit isn't entirely comfortable, because the general category here is "political parties," which exist to engage in activities at the heart of the First Amendment's concerns, but it's good enough to justify the kinds of state regulation of political parties to which we've become accustomed.

With these preliminaries out of the way, we can now look at how the states regulate political parties, and the limits the Supreme Court has placed on them. We'll start with a small issue—who gets on the ballot?—and move to increasingly important ones.

24. More jargon: To be constitutional, a content-based regulation has to serve a "compelling" government interest and be "narrowly tailored" to restrict only speech that impairs that interest.

25. These regulations used to be called "time, place, and manner" regulations, until constitutional scholars explained that they were permissible because they were neutral, not because they dealt with the time, place, or manner of speech. You sometimes still see the older term used, though.

Ballot access. Illinois Congressman John Anderson ran in the Republican presidential primaries in 1980 and got a fair amount of support from Rockefeller Republicans. The party had already changed, though, and Anderson peaked early and faded as Ronald Reagan and George H. W. Bush dominated the party primaries. Anderson dropped out of the Republican race and decided to run as an independent. Doing so required that he get on the ballot for the November election in as many states as possible. Every state has regulations about who can get on the ballot. The major parties always qualify, not because they are named in the regulations but because the regulations automatically put on the ballot a party that got a lot of votes in some recent election. Third parties have a harder row to hoe. They have to collect signatures from qualified voters and file them well before the election. Sometimes the required numbers are extremely high, and the timing requirements quite stringent.[26]

Anderson ran up against this problem in Ohio and other states. Ohio's ballot access rules required independent candidates to declare their candidacies in March of a presidential election year. But in March 1980 Anderson was still hoping to win the Republican nomination. He didn't announce his

26. Some states also tried to require that third parties hold expensive primary elections or conventions to select their candidates.

intention to run as an independent until late April. Ohio's election officials said that he couldn't get on that state's ballot. A lower court ordered that Anderson's name be put on the ballot (in November he got slightly more than 250,000 votes in Ohio, or about 6 percent). Eventually the Supreme Court ruled that Ohio's early-filing requirement was unconstitutional because it placed too severe a burden on the rights of people who wanted to vote for Anderson.[27]

Every fourth year there's a spate of litigation by third parties about ballot access. Generally speaking, though, the rules adopted in response to the Supreme Court's rulings make it possible for third parties to get on the ballot almost everywhere. Because European elections use proportional representation, we haven't yet seen the equivalents of the Beer Party that ran candidates in elections in Poland, or the Pirate Party ("piracy" on the Internet, not on the high seas) that won a few seats in elections in 2009 for the European Union parliament. Still, in the 2008 presidential election, three minor parties—the Green Party, the Constitution Party, and the Libertarian Party—and independent Ralph Nader were on the ballots in enough states to get the 270 electoral votes needed to become president. Any

27. The Supreme Court has upheld "sore loser" statutes that bar someone who ran and lost in a primary election from running as an independent. Anderson withdrew from the Ohio primary before the deadline under Ohio's "sore loser" statute.

reasonably serious third party can get on the ballot in the United States.

Third parties almost never win major elections, of course, although independents sometimes do.[28] Political scientists and historians argue, though, that third parties matter—at times—because they scare the major parties into altering their platforms. As a result the Supreme Court's ballot-access decisions do have some effects on what the major parties offer the American people.

Fusion candidacies and the two-party system. Of course, getting on the ballot doesn't mean much, given the strength of the two-party system. The Supreme Court's decisions make it clear that states can't keep third parties off the ballot simply because the states want to preserve the two-party system. In one important case, though, the Supreme Court turned back an effort to use the Constitution to weaken the two-party system.

The case involved a "fusion" campaign. Permitted in a handful of states, including New York, fusion campaigns operate this way. The major parties pick their candidates. A third party then nominates as its candidate one of the major party candidates, with that candidate's permission. The candidate's name

28. Putting aside anomalous cases like that of Senator Joseph Lieberman, the main recent examples are Representative and Senator Bernard Sanders of Vermont and Governor Jesse Ventura of Minnesota.

appears twice on the ballot, once for the major party and once for the third party. When the votes are counted, though, election officials ignore the party label and add up the votes for the candidate. Fusion candidacies are good for third parties because they can show the public—and the leaders of the major parties—that voters might like a particular candidate but not the major party. Like most states, Minnesota doesn't allow fusion candidacies. A candidate's name can appear twice, but the votes are counted under the party label. Minnesota's New Party said that these regulations denied its supporters their right to associate in support of the candidate they favored. The Supreme Court disagreed, with Chief Justice William Rehnquist writing, "States . . . have a strong interest in the stability of their party systems. . . . The Constitution permits [states] to decide that political stability is best served through a healthy two-party system."

States can choose to favor the two-party system. And it's hardly surprising that they do, given that the two major parties dominate state legislatures. Still, we shouldn't exaggerate the importance of the Supreme Court's decisions for the two-party system. Mostly we have a two-party system because of Duverger's Law—the tendency to have only two parties in systems with district-based elections in which the winner is the candidate with more votes than any other candidate—and because we have become accustomed to and are generally satisfied with the brands the major parties offer us.

Regulating candidate selection. What about state regulation of the parties themselves? Here the Court has interpreted the First Amendment to require that states pretty much take a hands-off stance. Parties can organize themselves and choose candidates however they want. Today, though, "parties" aren't quite what they used to be, and saying that the Constitution requires that "they" be allowed to organize themselves however they want has important implications for our party system.

According to the Supreme Court, the First Amendment prevents the states from overriding a party's choice of how to conduct its primary or convention. As Justice Antonin Scalia put it in a recent decision, "A political party has a First Amendment right to limit its membership as it wishes, and to choose a candidate-selection process that will in its view produce the nominee who best represents its political platform." This made sense when there really were parties of an old-fashioned sort, with party leaders, rules for membership, and the like. It's less clear that it makes sense today.

Still, often we have good reason to be suspicious of government efforts to impose candidate-selection rules on political parties, even those as loosely organized as contemporary American parties are.

A Connecticut case illustrates why. State Republican leaders decided that they could attract voters to their positions by allowing independents to vote in the Republican primary, thereby influencing who the Republican candidate in the general election would be. They thought that a candidate chosen in such an "open" primary might be more moderate than one chosen in a "closed" primary in which only registered Republicans could vote, and they welcomed that prospect because they thought that a moderate Republican would have a better chance of winning the general election. The leaders of the state's Democratic Party agreed with that political prediction, and they didn't like it. And they had the resources to fight it— not by running candidates who could beat a moderate Republican, but by getting the state legislature, which their party controlled, to enact a law saying that political parties had to run closed primaries. The Supreme Court told them that they couldn't structure the playing field to make it more likely that they would win.

Just to show you that something's going on here that's distinct from our usual ideas about the Court's conservative-liberal divides, the Court's opinion upholding what the state Republican Party wanted to do was written by Justice Thurgood Marshall and was joined by the Court's liberals, with the Court's conservatives in dissent. Justice Marshall's opinion acknowledged that contemporary political parties are complicated entities:

A major state political party necessarily includes individuals playing a broad spectrum of roles in the organization's activities. Some of the Party's members devote substantial portions of their lives to furthering its political and organizational goals, others provide substantial financial support, while still others limit their participation to casting their votes for some or all of the Party's candidates. Considered from the standpoint of the Party itself, the act of formal enrollment or public affiliation with the Party is merely one element in the continuum of participation in Party affairs, and need not be in any sense the most important.

Connecticut's lawyers said that requiring closed primaries prevented one party from "raiding" the other. Justice Marshall responded, "Of course. That's precisely the point—and 'raiding' is what we would otherwise call 'attracting new voters,' something the First Amendment protects." Answering Connecticut's argument that closed primaries protected the two-party system, Justice Marshall said that each party was entitled to decide for itself how it wanted to be one of the two parties in a two-party system. A political party "transiently enjoying majority power" can't use the legislature to tell the other party how it has to conduct its own affairs.

Fair enough. Parties can choose to run open or closed primaries. Closed primaries have their own problems—not necessarily from the parties' point of view, but from the point of view of the ordinary voter, who gets interested in politics only when the November election rolls around. And, unfortunately from that perspective, closed primaries have a self-reinforcing character that makes them difficult to displace after they have been used for a while. Only people who register as party members can vote in closed primaries. As I noted earlier, people who do that—what one Supreme Court justice called "the party faithful"—tend to be more active in party affairs than others. That's true even when, as is possible in many states, a voter can register as a party member—or even switch registrations—right up to the day of the primary election. And, among those who identify themselves as party members, the ones who take time to vote in a primary election tend to be those who are more devoted to the party's ideological agenda. We know what the effects are: Democratic candidates chosen in a closed primary are rather liberal, Republicans rather conservative. According to political scientists, closed primaries do tend to screen out candidates from the extremes of their parties, but as the parties have become more ideologically coherent (at least district by district and state by state), Democrats choose liberal candidates, Republicans conservative ones.

Nothing wrong with that, of course. The problem is that the electorate as a whole—not the party activists in both parties—would rather not have to be forced to choose between a rather conservative Republican and a rather liberal Democrat. Moderate voters would like a choice, not an echo, to quote Barry

Goldwater's campaign slogan, but a choice between a moderately conservative Republican and a moderately liberal Democrat. Closed primaries tend—it's only a tendency, but strong enough—to prevent them from having that choice.

The Connecticut case, ruling out a state law forcing parties to run closed primaries, implies that state legislatures can't force them to run open ones either. Note, though, that we could see partisan maneuvering at work when Connecticut's Democrats tried to tilt the playing field. Perhaps we should think about the problem differently if the voters themselves design the primary system. California's voters did just that in 1996, adopting an initiative that switched from closed primaries, not to open ones, but to what's known in the field as a "blanket" primary. In such a primary election, you walk into the polling booth and can vote for one of the Democrats seeking to run in the general election for governor and then for one of the Republicans seeking to run for senator. Blanket primaries have political effects like those of open primaries: They push candidate selection toward the middle. As the California initiative's supporters put it, the blanket primary "would 'weaken' party 'hard-liners' and ease the way for 'moderate problem-solvers.' "

Seven Supreme Court justices joined an opinion by Justice Antonin Scalia holding that this too was unconstitutional. The initiative "forces political parties to associate with—to have their nominees, and hence their positions, determined by—those who, at best, have refused to affiliate with the party, and, at worst, have expressly affiliated with a rival." Justice Scalia continued, "Such forced association has the likely outcome—indeed, in this case the *intended* outcome—of changing the parties' message. We can think of no heavier burden on a political party's associational freedom." Legislation couldn't take away from the parties their "basic function" of selecting their own leaders—an observation that, by giving "the party" a more concrete existence than it actually has in today's United States, may contribute to party polarization. The fact that the system was adopted by the voters directly rather than by a party-dominated legislature played no part in the Court's analysis.

There's one last possibility, used in Washington state and Louisiana: the so-called jungle primary, in which there's just one primary election. Each candidate in a jungle primary says that he or she will run in the general election as either a Democrat or a Republican. When the votes in the jungle primary are tallied, the winners are the self-identified Democrat and Republican who receive more votes than any other self-identified Democrat or Republican. The jungle primary has effects like those of open primaries in pushing candidates toward the middle. Although somewhat skeptical about the constitutionality of Washington's jungle primary, the Supreme Court in 2008 refrained from striking it down, pending the presentation of more detailed information about the actual effects of the primary on candidate selection.[29]

The Supreme Court's interpretations of the First Amendment tell lawmakers to keep their hands off of internal party organization so that "the parties" can decide for themselves whom they want to lead them and how they want to go about attracting votes. As the Connecticut case shows, this stance might make sense when we're dealing with laws adopted by legislatures, composed of politicians interested in preserving their own positions. It makes less sense for situations like California's use of an initiative to reform the party structure—although even there we shouldn't exaggerate the extent to which initiatives are truly nonpartisan lawmaking processes. The effects of the Court's interpretations are clear enough: No matter how dissatisfied we are with the choices made by the "party faithful," we're stuck with them—unless we ourselves become party faithfuls either within existing parties or in new ones. Many of us have

29. The Supreme Court had already held that federal statutes prohibit Louisiana's use of the jungle primary for selection of candidates for the Senate and the House of Representatives, but only because Louisiana set the primary date for October rather than November and said that a candidate who got more than a majority of the votes in October was automatically elected.

better things to do with our time, which means that we really are going to be stuck with what the parties choose.

The Special Problem of Campaign Finance and the First Amendment

The elephant in the room, of course, is campaign finance.[30] Here the jargon is almost suffocating: "527s," "issue ads or express advocacy," "leadership PACs," "bundlers"—these terms and many more pervade the law of campaign finance. But, again taking a wide view, we can say roughly this: As interpreted by the Supreme Court, the First Amendment allows modest regulation of contributions to candidates, relatively little regulation of contributions to groups that sponsor advertisements and the like effectively supporting or opposing particular candidates, no regulation of expenditures by candidates, and quite limited regulation of spending by anyone else.[31]

30. Other aspects of First Amendment law, such as the law restricting the ability of public officials to recover damages for false stories whose publication damages their reputations, affect our political structure generally, but not the role that political parties play within that structure. Similarly for some structural provisions in the Constitution. My argument is that what matters are political parties, and so I put to one side these other provisions, relevant to politics in general but not to political parties specifically.

31. Spending by candidates who accept public financing can be

Spending. It's hard to come up with good reasons for limiting campaign spending, except maybe that raising money for campaigns takes time that our politicians could better spend on developing good public policy. Moralists might say that we spend "too much" on political campaigns, just as they might say that we spend too much on fast food. Maybe we can make sense of the idea of spending too much on fast food by pointing out that eating too many Big Macs leads to obesity. It's not clear what harm there is from listening to too many campaign commercials, though. Perhaps some sort of generalized disillusionment with the political system, if the advertisements are too negative or focus too much on aspects of politics that moralists think shouldn't really matter? That concern, though, is probably best handled by limiting contributions to campaigns. Wholly apart from the First Amendment, a society that lets us choose between fast food and organic food almost certainly has to let us trade off some food for some campaign spending. As the Court put it in its most important campaign finance decision, "In the free society ordained by our Constitution it is not the government, but the people—individually as citizens and

---

limited as a condition of receiving the money—which is why the national system of public financing for presidential elections has broken down. Public financing at the state and local level might be easier to sustain because the amounts needed to finance campaigns at that level are significantly smaller, at least in some locations.

candidates and collectively as associations and political committees—who must retain control over the quantity and range of debate on public issues in a political campaign."[32] This isn't entirely satisfactory: Why can the people "collectively as associations and political committees" decide how much to spend on political campaigns but the people "collectively" through our legislatures cannot do the same? Yet, of course there's a fair amount of force to the idea underlying the Court's somewhat inept way of putting the point. The First Amendment simply nails down the proposition that spending money on campaigns is just like spending money on fast food.

More commonly, people get concerned not about the absolute level of campaign spending but about what they see as an unequal or unfair distribution of spending. The two major parties, they sometimes say, ought to spend roughly the same amount. The Supreme Court in a rather gross overstatement rejected equalization as a reason for limiting campaign spending, saying that "the concept that government may restrict the speech of some elements of our society in order to enhance the relative voice of others is wholly foreign to the First Amendment." For complex reasons not worth developing here, that's

32. The Court's opinion in this case was unsigned, but the drafts found in available records from Supreme Court justices' papers show that this passage came from Justice Potter Stewart.

not quite right either,[33] but again the basic perception is sound. Why should a candidate blathering on about really bad policy proposals necessarily get pretty much the same air time as his opponent who's seriously discussing the nation's real problems? Suppose the second candidate finds it easy to raise money for the smart, policy-oriented ads. Why should we worry if the first candidate can't do the same for the dumb ads?

These are policy arguments against trying to regulate campaign spending. The Supreme Court has inscribed them in the First Amendment. Do the Court's decisions matter? Probably not. Again, think of campaign finance rules as if they were the tax code. Rich people pay tax lawyers a lot of money to find loopholes to exploit in the tax code. Any system of regulating campaign spending would inevitably have loopholes too. Think here of a moderately expensive campaign video sent over the Internet, that then goes viral. Within the spending rules, perhaps, but raising the same concerns that unequal spending does. Legislatures that had the power, unrestricted by the Constitution, to regulate campaign spending almost certainly wouldn't have the ability to do so.

33. There's a body of First Amendment law, dealing with the right of demonstrators to use streets for marches, that can be understood only on the theory that relatively poor people can't afford to take out newspaper ads to get their ideas across to the public even though relatively rich people can.

Campaign contributions to candidates. To spend as much as you can on campaigns requires that you raise money. Millionaires can spend a lot of their own money to finance their campaigns, but when they run for a Senate seat, not to mention the presidency, they have to get money from other people. And ordinary politicians don't even have a lot of personal money to spend anyway.

Before dealing with the Supreme Court's decisions on campaign finance, we have to clear away one pretty bad argument that often comes up in discussions of campaign finance regulation. It's this: The First Amendment deals with government regulation of speech, but money isn't speech. The Constitution allows the government to regulate the way we use our money all the time: It prohibits us from spending our money to buy narcotics, for example, or from buying drugs that the Food and Drug Administration has found to be unsafe. Why can't it regulate the way we spend our money on political campaigns?

The starting point has to be the obvious proposition that if the First Amendment means anything, it means that the government can't stop me from standing in front of my house and making a speech supporting a political candidate. But suppose I'm not a very good speaker. It would be pretty outrageous if the government told me that I couldn't hire someone to deliver the speech. The step from hiring someone to make the speech to hiring someone to write the speech is also quite small. Which is to say that the First Amendment has to come into play when we use our money to support political candidates. "Come into play" doesn't mean that the government can't regulate our contributions, but it does mean that we can't dismiss the First Amendment's application to campaign finance regulations simply because "money isn't speech."

People give money to political candidates because they think that the candidate should be elected, and they think that the candidate should be elected because her positions on the most important issues are better than her opponent's positions. Or so it would be in the best of worlds. In our world, things are sometimes less rosy. I might give a candidate's campaign $500,000, asking for a promise in return that if elected the candidate will introduce or vote for some law I want enacted. This is a pretty straightforward bribe. The candidate gets something she wants—an increased chance of winning, which isn't quite the same as a new car—in exchange for doing something I want rather than exercising her best judgment about what's in the public's interest. We are, as the federal fraud statute puts it, being deprived of the official's "honest services." The Supreme Court has said that legislatures can limit campaign contributions to guard against the possibility of this sort of quid pro quo corruption.

Voters seem to be concerned about two other phenomena, which they tend to describe as corruption as well. On learning that an elected official received a total of millions of dollars in contributions from people associated with the oil and gas industry, or banks, or some other industry, ordinary voters tend to suspect that the official's support for legislation favoring the oil and gas industry, or banks, or whatever, might not result from an honest assessment of the proposal's merits but from gratitude and a hope of receiving similar contributions in the future. Here, too, ordinary voters tend to think that they are being deprived of honest services. Washington insiders, which includes Supreme Court justices, know that this interpretation of the contributions has the causal arrow backward. The donors don't give their contributions to candidates so as to influence their votes. They pick candidates to give money to by looking over the field and deciding which ones are likely to favor their interests if the candidates are elected. The contributions increase the chance that the candidates chosen will win and will then be able to implement the policy views favorable to the industry that they already have.[34] The Supreme Court has half-heartedly been willing to characterize this public concern as a form of corruption—"appearance of corruption" is the phrase sometimes used—justifying regulation of campaign contribu-

34. Sometimes people give money to candidates who don't have fixed views on the issues the donors are interested in, expecting to get access to the candidate after his election to explain why the industry's position makes sense.

tions. The Court clearly regards this as a weaker justification than the anti–quid pro quo corruption justification, though, and accordingly won't use it to justify stringent regulations of contributions.

Finally, some ordinary voters translate the amounts of money they see being spent on campaigns into a generalized cynicism about politics as a place where everything's got to be for sale. No Supreme Court decision has been willing to accept this cynicism as a justification for campaign finance regulation.

Experience with campaign finance regulation suggests that it might not make much difference. Consider the simplest version, restrictions on direct individual contributions to campaigns. The first thing worth noting is that these restrictions aren't nearly as tight as you might think. Here's a description of the individual contribution limits for the 2005–2006 election cycle.[35] "[A]n individual may give $2,100 per election to a federal candidate (primary and general elections count separately, for a total of $4,200 to a single congressional candidate in an election cycle). An individual may also contribute $26,700 per year to the national committee of a political party and $10,000 per year to the federal account of a state party

35. The limits go up slightly each year because of an inflation adjustment. They were higher for the 2008 presidential election, but the numbers I've quoted give a flavor of how the system actually works.

committee." That's $40,900 per year per person—and it doesn't include the $10,000 per year an individual can give to a "Levin" account, which uses the money for get-out-the-vote activities, or contributions to candidates' legal defense accounts. The amounts aren't unlimited, as they used to be, but they certainly are large enough to give rich people a significant role in funding campaigns.

And that's not all. If you get along with your spouse and children, they too can make contributions up to the same limits (from their "own" funds, of course) to the candidate you prefer. More important, you can become a "bundler." Bundlers ask their friends and acquaintances to make contributions up to the statutory limits, and the bundlers then collect the checks and send them in a batch to the campaign. The candidate's managers know who put the bundle together, and a bundler who delivers $150,000 in checks from a bunch of people probably has about as much influence today as the person who wrote a single check for $150,000 had in the days before campaign finance regulation.[36] Maybe all rich people don't have the same opportunities to "make" large contributions as they used to, but gregarious rich people do.

36. Stories in mid-2009 about President Obama's nominations for posts as ambassadors noted that some of the nominees had indeed been bundlers, just as some ambassadors in the past had given large individual contributions to campaigns.

All this happens within the constraints the Supreme Court has put on campaign finance regulation. It's hard to believe that those constraints matter a great deal, that is, that things could be much worse, if the Court said that the First Amendment placed no limits at all on regulation of campaign contributions —at least to those ordinary voters who see an appearance of corruption in the campaign finance system or who have become cynical about politics because of campaign finance scandals. Maybe voters would be able to get our representatives to impose more stringent limits on campaign contributions (and expenditures) if we were able to tell them that according to the Supreme Court the First Amendment didn't have any bearing on their choices. I personally wouldn't bet on it.

And to some extent, that's a good thing. Debating whether to adopt the McCain-Feingold Act, many senators—Senator Mitch McConnell (R-Ky.) being the most prominent—regularly argued that the proposal's restrictions on campaign finance violated the First Amendment. Those arguments didn't go away merely because the Court upheld the statute against McConnell's challenge. Members of Congress have and sometimes honor the duty to consider the constitutionality of the proposals they weigh, and some of them sometimes think that that duty requires that they come to a judgment about constitutionality independent of what the Supreme Court will say, or even what it has said. The First Amendment, as those sen understand it, might affect the legislation that gets out of Congress, even if the Supreme Court said that in its view the First Amendment didn't limit what Congress could do.

"Independent" expenditures, issue advertising, and contributions supporting them. Suppose you think that Senator Smith has done just a terrific job and deserves to be reelected. We know that Congress can limit the amount you can contribute to Senator Smith's campaign. So, once you've hit the limits, you decide to spend your money buying an advertisement.[37] Obviously, you can't call up Senator Smith's campaign offices and tell them that you'll buy time to put whatever advertisement they choose on the air, because that would be a transparent evasion of the limits on campaign contributions. In the jargon, you can't coordinate your spending with the campaign. You can make a truly independent expenditure, though. And lots of the time you'll be able to hire a political consultant who isn't working for Senator Smith's campaign who can make a good advertisement that fits well with the themes Senator Smith has been articulating in her campaign. The same logic that gives First

37. Political action committees (PACs) and "527s"—named after the provision of the Internal Revenue Code that describes them—are vehicles for groups of people to aggregate their individual contributions so that they can make more effective and more numerous independent ads.

Amendment protection to your speech favoring Senator Smith leads to the conclusion that the First Amendment protects independent expenditures supporting a candidate.

Truly independent expenditures pose some risks to the candidate. Senator Smith might have calculated that she would have a better chance of winning the election if her campaign didn't make a point of presenting her position against gun control, for example. You might agree with her position against gun control but disagree with her calculation about the effect of raising that issue on her chances of winning, and distribute an advertisement praising her for opposing gun control. Then she might have to address an issue that she herself didn't want to address. Overall, though, independent expenditures are going to help far more candidates than they hurt. They also undermine any system of campaign finance regulation—but it's really hard to come up with a sensible interpretation of the First Amendment that would allow government to regulate independent expenditures by individuals.

As the modern system of campaign finance regulation took hold, the United States saw a proliferation of "issue advertising." An issue ad takes a position on some issue—drilling for oil, health care, filibusters in the Senate—that its sponsor thinks has some immediate political resonance. Suppose, for example, that it's the summer of an election year and the Senate is considering legislation dealing with health care financing. Senator Smith has made some statements suggesting that she's open to including a provision taxing the amount an employer contributes for health insurance for employees who make more than $250,000 a year. People who think that's a bad idea sponsor an issue ad urging Senator Smith to oppose the provision.

Issue ads seem to be a pristine form of political communication. What's special about them? It's this: Corporations and unions are prohibited from making any contributions whatsoever to a candidate's campaign. They can sponsor issue ads, though. The McCain-Feingold campaign finance act treated some issue ads as what it called "electioneering communications"—more jargon—which it defined as any ad broadcast within sixty days of a general election. It extended to electioneering communications the existing ban on corporate and union financial contributions to candidates. Corporations couldn't make contributions for issue ads aired shortly before an election. Congress's concern was, once again, that issue ads could be used to evade the ban on corporate contributions to candidates. Adopting an extremely narrow definition of what sorts of ads endorse candidates the Supreme Court held this provision unconstitutional as applied to an issue ad that wasn't unmistakably an endorsement, in an opinion by Chief Justice John Roberts. In a portion of his opinion joined only by Justice Samuel Alito, the

Chief Justice wrote, "Enough is enough. Issue ads . . . are by no means equivalent to contributions, and the *quid-pro-quo* corruption interest cannot justify regulating them." The "issue ad" case didn't involve what specialists in campaign finance regulation call express advocacy—an ad whose only reasonable interpretation is that it urges voters to support or oppose a particular candidate. (As I write, the Court seems poised to sharply limit Congress's power to regulate express advocacy by corporation.)

Corporations and unions can use their treasuries to buy issue ads and engage in express advocacy. Sometimes they do so in their own names, but more often they make contributions to— or set up—fronts with innocuous names like "Citizens for Responsible Whatever." They do have to disclose their contributions, and some advocates of campaign reform have begun to argue for instant disclosures on the Web. There's one important difference between contributions from corporate and union treasuries, though. The Supreme Court has held that the First Amendment requires that unions inform their members that each one has a right to insist that none of his or her union dues be spent on political activity. Stockholders don't have an equivalent right. The theory is that a stockholder who doesn't like what the corporation's managers are doing with the corporate treasury can simply "exit" the corporation by selling the shares, whereas in unionized workplaces every worker is required to pay union dues. The Supreme Court hasn't been troubled by the asymmetry it's created between unions and corporations.[38]

Here we have arrived at a place where the Constitution—as interpreted by the Supreme Court, of course—matters. Its campaign finance decisions, in particular, probably make it difficult for us not merely to alter our system of campaign finance, but to change the overall structure of our party system—if we wanted to.

Again, though, there are some structural features of the national Constitution that may be more important than the Court's decisions interpreting the First Amendment. On the national level, there's no provision for direct legislation by the people. Many observers deride the widespread use of direct legislation—the initiative and referendum—in California and other states. Direct legislation is a good tool, though, in one specific area—regulation of politics. It has the potential to allow the people to work around the politicians they've elected to do *other* kinds of work. When politicians turn to regulating politics, perhaps we should worry. Which is to say: Even if the

38. Victor Brudney, a prominent scholar of corporation law, has argued for nearly a generation that the government ought to impose on corporations a requirement that they obtain specific permission from shareholders—even unanimous consent, he has suggested—for expenditures on issue ads and especially express advocacy. His campaign has made no progress, though.

Court interpreted the First Amendment to allow Congress to do whatever it wanted, perhaps we should worry.

Consider campaign finance laws, which—on the national level—must be adopted by Congress. Many scholars suspect that those laws are incumbent protection rackets. Members of Congress figure out where the money to finance opponents comes from, and try to limit that money without limiting the money they can raise.[39] The most spectacular example may be the "Millionaires' Amendment" in the McCain-Feingold law. The provision said that if you were running against someone who put a lot of his or her own money on the line—$350,000 or more—you were freed of the ordinary limits on campaign contributions: You could accept individual contributions of up to three times the ordinary limits. But, of course, millionaires who run for office use not only their own money. They raise additional funds by accepting contributions from others. The Millionaires' Amendment said that "self-financing" candidates had to abide by the ordinary limits. An incumbent facing a self-financing candidate was freed of restrictions placed on his or her opponent. In 2008, the Supreme Court struck down the Millionaires' Amendment, dividing along standard conservative-liberal lines.

39. The opponents might be insurgents within their own parties, or the candidates who run against them in the general election.

That case shows that the Court's intervention can have some, almost certainly modest, effect on the use of campaign finance law to entrench incumbents. Reelection rates for the House and Senate are quite high, and the incumbents' advantages flow in part from their ability to outraise and outspend their opponents. Only in part, though: Voters can be swayed by campaign advertising,[40] but most of the time we vote for our incumbents because on the whole we approve of what they've been doing and aren't sure that any replacement will be better for us.

Suppose the Supreme Court said that the First Amendment prohibited any limitations on campaign finance: Corporations could use company money to support candidates, rich people could give as much money as they wanted to any many candidates as they wanted, labor unions could use membership dues for campaign contributions. Campaign finance would be a free-for-all—or, more accurately, a pay-if-you-can. "The market" would determine who got how much. Perhaps I'm overly cynical, but I find it hard to believe that things would be much different from the way they are today, or even from the way they would be if the Court interpreted the First Amendment to

40. Most political scientists who have studied the matter think that negative advertising is particularly effective—and doesn't seem to have the effect of lowering public expectations about or respect for politicians or the political system.

place no limits on what legislatures—politicians, that is—can do to regulate campaign finance. The Court itself has referred to what campaign finance scholars call the "hydraulic" theory of campaign finance: Try as hard as you can, you'll still have a system with cracks through which money will first seep and then flood. The experience in other nations isn't all that encouraging. The British Labour Party was hit with a scandal about selling seats in the House of Lords in exchange for campaign contributions, for example. And then there's Italy's Prime Minister Silvio Berlusconi, who parlayed his immense wealth into a political career. Even if the Court said that we could regulate campaign finance however we wanted, afterward we might find ourselves as dissatisfied as we were when we began.

There's one final point, this one about the Supreme Court. To simplify the argument developed in more detail in Chapter Two: The Supreme Court interprets the Constitution the way it does because it too is both a part and the result of our political system. Making some concessions for time lags and similar glitches, we can expect the Court's interpretations to reinforce the constitutional positions most consistent with those of the then-dominant political regime. The clearest example I've presented so far is the Court's endorsement of the two-party system in the Minnesota fusion case. The most problematic example is the Court's position on campaign fir ~e regulation, although Chapter Two will present some argi that might help us understand why it might not be inconsistent with politicians' preferences for the Court to strike down campaign finance statutes the politicians themselves have enacted.

The overall lesson is reasonably clear: Put politicians in charge of campaign finance, and they'll enact laws that reinforce the existing structure of politics. Put judges in charge, and they'll interpret the Constitution to—aha!—reinforce the existing structure of politics.

Conclusion

The preceding section has discussed how the Supreme Court's constitutional interpretations shape the contours of our politics. That shouldn't be taken to suggest that the Constitution matters to our politics because of what the Supreme Court has said. Far more important are the structural features—the separation of powers and federalism, for example—that affect the way parties are organized. The features are of course in the Constitution. So of course the Constitution matters, primarily because of these structural features. I turn to the Supreme Court in the next chapter, to examine how the Supreme Court matters. We will see why politics matters there too.

2

how the supreme court matters

Suppose the Supreme Court overruled *Roe v. Wade* (or substitute whatever important Supreme Court opinion you want). One day women all over the country had a right to choose to have an abortion if that was what they wanted. The next day women in some, perhaps many, states wouldn't have that right. Obviously this is a situation in which the Constitution matters. Or so it would seem.

Appearances are deceiving—or perhaps more precisely, the example shows not that the Constitution matters but that the Supreme Court does. And even that isn't so clear when we start to think about the example in detail. Because, after all, five justices don't simply happen to wake up one morning and say to themselves, "Whoops, our predecessors made a big mistake in 1973. We ought to do something about that." I'll provide details to qualify the following quite crude explanation for a decision like the one we're imagining, but the crude account helps frame this chapter. Five justices decide to overrule *Roe v. Wade* because one or more presidents nominated them knowing that their general orientation to constitutional interpretation would make them quite skeptical about *Roe,* and hoping that that skepticism would eventually lead them to overrule *Roe.* And the presidents nominated them because they calculated that they would gain political advantages from some important constituencies by nominating justices of that sort. The general story has political constituencies (sometimes scholars call them social movements) influencing presidents, presidents choosing justices in response to those constituencies, and justices interpreting the Constitution in ways the constituencies favor.

Politics determines when the Supreme Court matters. And the politics of the Supreme Court has some patterns—not rigid "laws of politics," but tendencies that help make sense of a lot of the Court's history. These patterns are connected to the ideas about regimes, presidential leadership, political parties, and divided or unified government that we examined in Chapter

One. We'll start with the simplest pattern, which is probably the most important one historically, and after unpacking why the pattern occurs move on to more complicated patterns.

The Supreme Court and Unified Government

Alexander Hamilton, a founder, and Alexander Bickel, a prominent modern constitutional scholar, offered two of the most famous statements about the Supreme Court. Writing what we would now call a newspaper opinion piece aimed at persuading New York's voters to support the proposed Constitution, Hamilton tried to allay concerns that the new Supreme Court created under the Constitution would be too powerful. Hamilton pointed out that the new Court would have "no influence over either the sword or the purse; no direction either of the strength or of the wealth of the society. . . . It may truly be said to have neither FORCE nor WILL, but merely judgment; and must ultimately depend upon the aid of the executive arm even for the efficacy of its judgments." Hamilton seems to be saying that the new courts won't be effective unless they persuade politicians to go along with them. Their opinions may contain reasons that politicians will pay attention to—but of course politicians pay attention to a lot more than that. The problem Hamilton finessed—or perhaps consciously suppressed, because he was writing with a specific political purpose himself—was this:

What if the politician's constituents don't find the Court's reasons convincing? Hamilton seems to say that when that happens the Court's decision won't have any effects on the ground. Or, from the politician's point of view, what the Court has to say is a datum to take into account in figuring out what's in the politician's best interests, but the Court's action isn't the last word on the subject.

Alexander Bickel, writing in 1957, reflecting on a century and a half of experience in the United States with Supreme Court constitutional interpretations, coined the phrase "countermajoritarian difficulty" to describe what the Supreme Court did. According to Bickel, the Supreme Court was an "anomalous" institution in our democracy, because a handful of unelected officials, with no direct responsibility to the people, had the power to override decisions made by democratically elected representatives—or, when they dealt with laws adopted by popular initiatives or referenda, decisions made by the people themselves. For Bickel, the Supreme Court was somehow above politics, not only because its opinions weren't supposed to be influenced by narrow political considerations but, more important, because its decisions *governed*—regulated or superseded—the decisions made by politicians.

An obvious tension exists between Bickel's perspective and Hamilton's. One way to see the tension is to ask, Why would a politician put up with judicial review exercised in the way

Bickel describes it? After all, the Supreme Court doesn't have the power of the purse or the sword, and it would seem as if Hamilton thought that a politician could safely ignore a Court decision she disagreed with.[1]

The answer, obvious to any politician, is that politicians put up with judicial review because they find it helpful to them politically. Helpful overall, that is, even if a Court decision will occasionally cause them some difficulties.

So, how can the Supreme Court help politicians? The most general answer is that it can do things the politicians themselves can't do even though the politicians might want (in some sense) to do them. Here the best entry point is to think about a Supreme Court during a period of extended unified government —when a political regime has been in place for a while and seems pretty solidly entrenched. The model to have in mind is the New Deal/Great Society Supreme Court—or, to use a more conventional term that obscures the political dynamics, the Warren Court in its heyday.

The Warren Court was an instrument of the New Deal/ Great Society political regime. Law professor L.A. Powe has given us the most astute detailed analysis of the way the Warren Court meshed with that political regime. According to Powe,

1. More precisely: A Court decision that she thought enough constituents disagreed with to make it politically sensible to oppose the Court rather than go along with it.

most of the Warren Court's decisions can be accounted for by seeing them as falling within several categories. Again, we can examine the simplest category, try to understand why politicians use the courts to deal with problems in that category, and then look at the mechanism politicians employ, before turning to more complex categories.

Sometimes the Warren Court placed local "outliers" under rules that were widespread and widely approved of throughout the nation. *Griswold v. Connecticut* invalidated that state's criminal law banning the use of contraceptives, even by married couples and even when prescribed by a physician. At the time Connecticut was only one of two states with such a law on the books.[2] And a lot of the Warren Court's work involved similar statutes—on the books in a few states but not really approved by the national majority on whose behalf the Warren Court was working.

It's worth pausing here to observe that we could understand this treatment of localized outliers in several ways.

---

2. My experience in talking to nonspecialist audiences about *Griswold* leads me to emphasize that Connecticut really did make it a crime to *use* contraceptives. It never prosecuted people for using them, of course. *Griswold* was a prosecution of a clinic operator for "aiding and abetting" the illegal use by distributing contraceptives to married couples whose doctors prescribed them.

- *Nationalism versus states' rights.* Warren Court liberals were (are?) also nationalists rather than federalists. They tend to think that the rules that regulate our personal lives should be pretty much the same everywhere in the country. The fact that the Warren Court was overriding a law that might have had the support of a local majority in the name of a national one wouldn't bother nationalists. They wouldn't even see this is as "counter" majoritarian at all, because for them the national majority is the only one that counts.

- *Overcoming perceived political blockages.* Another way of understanding the problem the Warren Court had with Connecticut refers directly to politics. Relying on other scholars' work, Powe shows that efforts to repeal Connecticut's ban on contraceptives were blocked by politicians who either agreed with the position taken by the state's Catholic bishops or felt that their seats were at risk if they disagreed with that position. Liberals interpreted this to suggest that under "normal" political conditions a majority of Connecticut's voters wouldn't actually support the contraceptive ban. Making sense of the word "normal" here is tricky and probably can't be done in any defensible way. Liberals of the 1960s weren't concerned about that. As they saw things, a decision like *Griswold* wasn't countermajoritarian even in local terms, because the real local majority—were it given a fair shot—would have gotten the law off the books. On this view the Warren Court was actually helping the real local majority, which faced unfair obstacles in the local political process.

- *"Backwaters."* A final way of understanding the treatment of outliers like Connecticut is that they are backwaters that haven't yet been reached by the national trends that swept over other states. Given enough time, Connecticut would have gotten around to repealing the ban on using contraceptives. All the Supreme Court did was push the day of repeal forward a bit. Here the Court's action is countermajoritarian in the short run, but promajoritarian in the long run—at least if the Court's prediction about national trends and their local effects is correct.

In all these variants most politicians—certainly on the national level, and perhaps locally as well—"wanted" to get rid of the laws on the books in outlier states because of their commitment to New Deal and Great Society principles. Why did they leave the job to the Supreme Court? Mostly because the politicians had other things, more important things as they saw it, to do with their time (and partly because it took them some time to figure out that they had the constitutional tools to displace state laws themselves). They had to develop the national system of labor law, design and implement a social security system, deal with international crises, and much more. They assigned the job of cleaning up the statute books to the Supreme Court.[3]

Griswold involved a statute that was a "geographical" outlier. There are also what we might call "temporal" outliers—old statutes that were enacted before the present, stable regime was established. These statutes could not be enacted in the new regime, but it's hard to repeal them. Partly that's because new regimes never completely eliminate representatives of the older order. Lyndon Johnson had large Democratic majorities in the House and the Senate, but the majorities weren't overwhelming. Opponents of the Great Society still occupied strategic positions in Congress. They couldn't enact anything on their own, but they could obstruct some initiatives. Laws already on the books are good subjects for that sort of obstruction. Repealing old laws is difficult as well, for the same reason that

3. There's one area of constitutional law, involving the so-called dormant commerce clause, whose doctrinal structure—as distinct from political context—is best understood as relying on this sort of congressional use of the courts. Thought important because it deals with the ability of state governments to regulate corporations that operate on a national scale, the area is quite technical, and it's not worth elaborating on the doctrine here.

disciplining geographical outliers is. It takes time and political energy that can be devoted to other, more important tasks. So, again, politicians use the courts to clean up the statute books. After some hesitation, the Warren Court found First Amendment violations in a fair number of laws enacted in the 1940s and 1950s to deal with the perceived threat of the domestic Communist Party and its allies. By the 1960s and 1970s these statutes were temporal anomalies, which almost certainly could not have been enacted then but which Congress could not get around to repealing. Liberal politicians were happy to discover that the Warren Court was willing to do a job they wanted done but couldn't do politically.

On an almost comically lower level is the quite limited "Federalism Revolution" of the Rehnquist Court's last years. Before Republicans took control of the House and the Senate the Rehnquist Court struck down one statute on the ground that it invaded state prerogatives.[4] After 1994 came some more invalidations. The poster child for the Federalism Revolution was a decision striking down a statute making it a federal crime to possess a gun near a school—a statute resulting from political grandstanding by Senator Herbert Kohl (D-Wis.), and one that the Republican Congress would never have adopted. So too

4. The Burger Court invalidated another statute on federalism grounds, but that decision was overruled within a few years.

with the handful of other decisions that were part of the feeble Federalism Revolution. The Supreme Court did a bit of spot cleaning of the statute books, getting rid of statutes that could not have been enacted after 1994.

Politicians make one additional use of the Supreme Court. Reconstructive presidents transform the nation's political institutions, in the face of prior constitutional doctrine that sometimes stands in their way. Once a reconstructive regime becomes resilient and stable, presidents need to get rid of the old, now truly obsolete doctrine. Once they get control of the Supreme Court, their appointees bring doctrine into line with the regime's new principles. That is how the Constitution came to accommodate the expansion of national power that accompanied the New Deal. This has a flip side. As a regime degenerates astute politicians might foresee their impending loss of power in Congress and the presidency, and can take advantage of whatever vacancies occur to write an insurance policy for the public policies they have managed to enact, by seeing that the courts are staffed by relatively young justices who will find unconstitutional efforts by the new regime to transform those policies. The insurance policy can't last forever, of course, but preserving the collapsed regime for a while in the courts might be the best these politicians can do.

Almost by definition "outliers" aren't all that important to the nation as a whole, no matter how difficult they may make life in one or another state. Some scholars have extended the idea, though, to cover cases where there's a substantial minority of states pursuing a policy that a national majority believes unconstitutional. One example is southern segregation before *Brown v. Board of Education.* Public opinion surveys in the early 1950s indicated that a national majority did not approve of segregation. In political terms African Americans in the urban North were an increasingly important component of the New Deal coalition. Segregation resulted from and helped sustain the political dominance of conservative white politicians in the Democratic Party in the South. Eliminating segregation would have strengthened liberals within the party by adding African American voices and votes to the party in the South. The Court's members at the time were political sophisticates and tended to be relatively liberal on issues of race. Hugo Black had been a senator, Robert Jackson had been Roosevelt's attorney general and a close personal adviser. Even justices obscure today were political major leaguers before they were appointed to the Court: Sherman Minton a senator, Harold Burton a celebrated reform mayor of Cleveland and senator. When Robert Jackson asked during the Court's deliberations over the segregation cases why the Court was being asked to find it unconstitutional if a national majority opposed the policy and could in theory get Congress to act, he knew the answer. The one-party Democratic South combined with the use of seniority in Congress to place long-sitting southerners, who could be reelected without opposition, in strategic positions within Congress that allowed them to block antisegregation legislation.

Scholars have generalized the approach I've just sketched. Politicians and judges, they argue, respond more to the policy and constitutional views of the nation's elites than to the views of its voters. Voters place some constraints on what elites can do, but mostly elites get their way. So, if the nation's elites opposed segregation, as they undoubtedly did, so will the Court. Or, more recently, if the nation's elites support gay and lesbian rights more strongly that the nation's voters do, so will the Court.

There's undoubtedly something to these stories, but I think they oversimplify things. They downplay the importance of ideological commitments associated with political regimes and focus too narrowly on immediate political concerns. The ideals of equality associated with the New Deal had something to do with *Brown,* for example. And, most generally, elite-driven explanations threaten to explain too much. If the Court invalidates an unpopular policy, it's simply acting against an outlier. If it invalidates a popular one, it's simply doing what the nation's elites want. If the Court acts against the views of a good chunk of the American people and of elites, it's simply acting on behalf of a narrow political interest (think here of *Bush v. Gore,* with five conservative justices awarding the presidency to

George W. Bush after an election that divided the nation and its elites evenly). There's nothing you can't explain in this way.

Before getting to more complicated scenarios, we should pick up on the hints I've already offered to explain how the patterns I've sketched come about.

The Politics of Judicial Selection

The basic mechanism that connects the Supreme Court to politics is of course the process of judicial nomination and selection. The Constitution gives the president the power to nominate Supreme Court justices, and the Senate the responsibility for voting to confirm the nominations. That means that the judicial selection process is political to the core. Presidents pick nominees to satisfy political demands on them, and senators vote to support or oppose confirmation to satisfy the sometimes different political demands they face.

This doesn't mean that the politics of judicial nominations has been the same throughout our history. What it means is that the politics of judicial nominations mirrors whatever else is happening in politics at the time. On the broadest level the political processes of judicial nominations are the same as whatever processes characterize policy-making at the time. And those processes change over time, although at every point in our history we can see examples of older processes.

- *Short-term politics.* Sometimes presidents use nominations to achieve short-term political goals. In 1956 President Dwight Eisenhower, a Republican, had to fill a vacancy while he was running for reelection. He and his advisers wanted to shore up his support among urban Catholics in the Northeast, so he nominated New Jersey Supreme Court Justice William Brennan, a Catholic, for the position. Short-term politics is usually a minor factor in the nomination process, though, because Supreme Court vacancies open up pretty much at random. Although every president always faces some short-term political problems, only a few of them can be eased by a Supreme Court nomination, and the president might not be facing one of those special kinds of problems when a vacancy occurs. It's hard to see short-term politics at work in the nomination of Stephen Breyer by Bill Clinton or the nomination of John Roberts by George W. Bush, for example.
- *Patronage.* In the 1880s, politics was dominated by patronage, with government structured around parties as dispensers of patronage. And so Supreme Court nominations were patronage appointments. Perhaps the most dramatic example, obscure today, is the Senate's rejection of President Ulysses S. Grant's nomination of Ebenezer Hoar to a Supreme Court vacancy. Hoar was

eminently qualified, having served as a state supreme court judge in Massachusetts and as Grant's attorney general. Still, the Republican-dominated Senate rejected Republican President Grant's nominee because Senate leaders wanted the position to go to someone associated with their faction within the Republican Party. More recently patronage has morphed into the politics of representation.

- *The politics of representation.* Throughout our history presidents have used Supreme Court nominations to ensure that politically important interests (to them) are represented on the Court. For much of the nation's history the most important dimension of representation was regional. Presidents wanted to make sure that people throughout the country could realistically think that the president and his party represented them, and one way of sending that message was to maintain regional representation on the Supreme Court. Franklin Roosevelt chose to nominate Wiley Rutledge in 1943 in large part because, unlike other candidates for nomination, Rutledge, who grew up in New Mexico and Colorado, was seen as a westerner.

Regional representation disappeared as a concern by the end of the twentieth century, but other dimensions of representation remained important. It's hard to imagine a Supreme Court in the rest of the twenty-first century without at least one woman and probably more, without an African American, and now without someone of Hispanic origin. Religion used to matter, at least to the extent that people could talk about a "Jewish" and a "Catholic" seat or two on the Court, but today religious representation seems to have disappeared from view.[5]

· *Ideology.* Readers familiar with recent judicial nominations probably think—correctly—that today nominations are about judicial ideology. Presidents and senators ask themselves, Is this candidate for appointment a judicial conservative or a judicial liberal? The focus on ideology is a relatively recent development. Its emergence is tied once again to the politics of the nomination process. Seeing the Great Society regime become vulnerable, Republican candidates starting with Barry Goldwater calculated that "running against the Court" was one component of a winning political strategy. They presented voters with their constitutional vision, quite distinct from the Warren Court's. And, once

5. At present the Supreme Court has six members who are Catholics, two who are Jews, and only one Protestant—a remarkable achievement in light of both the nation's history and its current demographic composition.

elected, they followed through as best they could—that is, within the political constraints they faced.

Here we have to return to issues of party structure in successive political regimes. From Richard Nixon through George W. Bush the Republican Party gradually became more ideologically homogeneous and conservative. Richard Nixon chose his nominees from a party with a significant northeastern, Nelson Rockefeller faction, at least moderate and probably reasonably liberal on issues like race discrimination and sexual privacy. And he was president when Democrats controlled the Senate. The result: Nixon focused on narrow political considerations in making his choices for the Supreme Court. To strengthen the Republican Party in the South, he looked for a southerner and, after his choices of a judge from South Carolina and one from Florida fell flat, chose corporate lawyer and Virginian Lewis F. Powell—for representation reasons, not because Powell satisfied stringent ideological criteria (he didn't; he was a rather conservative Democrat, not an ideological partisan). Nixon had campaigned on a platform of strengthening what he called the "peace forces," that is, the police, and he nominated justices whom he thought, accurately, would generally rule against criminal defendants raising constitutional claims.

As the Republican Party grew more conservative, Republican presidents no longer had to satisfy the remnants of the party's northeastern wing. They could confine their attention to nominees whom, they thought, were likely to be reliably conservative. And, on the whole, that's what they did. President Reagan's one failure—the nomination of Robert Bork, defeated in the Senate—occurred, again, during divided government when Democrats controlled the Senate (and when Reagan, in his second and final term, had been politically weakened by the then ongoing scandal about trading arms for the contra rebels in Nicaragua in exchange for the release of hostages by groups affiliated with Iran).

The Democratic Party did not move as decisively or as quickly to ideological homogeneity. Bill Clinton, the only Democrat with an opportunity to nominate a justice between 1968 and 2009, understood that he was operating within the constraints of the Reagan Revolution, with important factions in his party supporting a relatively conservative political agenda. He nominated two justices, both "liberals" when assessed against the Court's overall composition but quite moderate when compared to the Warren Court's liberals.

Surrounding the parties are interest groups. Traditional interest groups sometimes played an important role in Supreme Court nominations. Labor unions joined with the National Association for the Advancement of Colored People to defeat President Herbert Hoover's nomination of Judge John J. Parker in 1930, for example. Generally, though, those interest groups stood in the background. The gradual transformation of the parties in the final twenty-five years of the last century produced a new type of interest group, organized to promote an ideology rather than the pocketbook interests of its supporters. Starting with the Bork nomination in 1987, ideological interest groups conducted vigorous campaigns around Supreme Court nominations. Their effects are unclear; the Bork nomination failed because of generally unfavorable political circumstances for President Reagan, and the interest-group attacks on Judge Bork might not have made much difference. But, as the parties became increasingly homogeneous, ideological interest groups found that judicial nominations were a useful focus for their fund-raising efforts and perhaps for some public education.

The Myths of Qualifications and Mistakes

We can't accurately describe the real-world politics of judicial nominations without paying attention to politics—sometimes short-term politics, as with Eisenhower's nomination of Brennan, sometimes long-term ones, as with the recent upsurge of concern about judicial ideology or philosophy.

Some politicians and their acolytes in the press and (unfortunately) in the academy pretend that there's something called "qualifications"—ability and character, mostly—that ought to be the sole focus in the nomination process. They pretend that presidents look only for nominees who are "qualified," and choose the "best" qualified person who comes to their attention. That happened—once—in the twentieth century, when President Herbert Hoover nominated Benjamin Cardozo. After that, nothing. The nadir of this pretense was President George H. W. Bush's statement, probably inadvertent, that Clarence Thomas was the most qualified person for a position on the Supreme Court when he was chosen in 1991. Thomas was clearly qualified in some basic sense, and he's been a solid performer as a Supreme Court justice, but it was silly to say then, as it would be silly to say now, that he was the best qualified person available for the position. Statements that the nomination process should be concerned only with qualifications are themselves positions taken to advance a political agenda. There's nothing wrong with that, but the statements should never be understood as resting on some politically neutral analysis of what our constitutional system requires.

Journalists sometimes focus on cases where president were supposedly surprised by what the justices they appointed did. Mistakes and surprises are quite rare. Presidents who pay attention usually get what they were looking for in Supreme Court nominees. What journalists describe as "surprises" occur, mostly, when presidents haven't been looking for political benefits flowing from a nominee's ideological commitments.

The modern examples journalists use are Earl Warren and

William Brennan, liberals nominated by the more conservative Dwight Eisenhower; Harry Blackmun, who became more liberal over time; and David Souter. In fact, Eisenhower knew what he was getting ideologically when he nominated Warren and Brennan—the former a Republican with a long track record as a progressive within the Republican Party, the latter a northern urban liberal Democrat. At the time of the nominations, though, Eisenhower cared more about other political benefits flowing from the nominations than about ideology. Indeed, Eisenhower had positioned himself within the Republican Party as someone who accepted the basic premises of Franklin Roosevelt's New Deal, and Warren and Brennan were committed to the New Deal's constitutional vision too. Something similar can be said about Souter; anyone who paid attention to his background, not to mention what he actually said during his confirmation hearings, would have understood that Souter was a northeastern liberal Republican.[6] It's just that the Republican Party pretty much shed that wing of the party between Souter's nomination and his retirement. Harry Blackmun is probably the only real case of an appointment that turned out to be a surprise, and even there the story is more

6. John Sununu, Bush's chief of staff who probably knew better, sold Souter as a conservative to conservatives, almost certainly (in my view) because Sununu understood that Souter's nomination was a done deal anyway.

complicated. President Richard Nixon nominated Blackmun as a law-and-order judge, and for much of Blackmun's career he was a reliable vote to uphold police practices against constitutional challenges. And, with respect to what became Blackmun's signature issue, abortion, it's important to remember that a significant component of the Republican Party when Nixon nominated Blackmun was the "country club Republican" faction, who were not uncomfortable with and often supported abortion rights.

Justices rarely surprise the presidents who appointed them on the issues the presidents paid attention to. Not so on other issues, for two reasons.

- *Times and political parties change.* Supreme Court justices serve as long as they want to. Presidents don't. As the example of the modern Republican Party shows, political parties change—sometimes substantially, and sometimes when the Supreme Court has quite a few justices, even a majority, appointed by a president from the party in its earlier incarnation. Today's party members might be disappointed at what "their" party's appointees are doing. That doesn't necessarily mean that presidents from their party made mistakes; it could mean that the party is different today from what it was when the appointments occurred.

- *Packages.* Presidents nominate people whom they believe will be reliable on the issues they care most about. Franklin Roosevelt wanted justices who would endorse the expansion of national power associated with the New Deal. He didn't care much about the positions his nominees would take on questions of civil rights and civil liberties. He couldn't have cared and still nominated both Frank Murphy, extremely liberal on such questions, and James Byrnes, a standard racist southern politician of the time. Both men were reliable New Dealers, though, on issues of national power, and that's what Roosevelt wanted. As it turned out, however, most (not all) reliable New Dealers were also reasonably liberal on questions of civil rights and civil liberties. And so the Roosevelt Court laid the foundation for the Warren Court's liberalism, not because that was what Roosevelt sought to accomplish but as a side effect of what he successfully achieved.

The politics of judicial nominations is the politics of the time, whatever it happens to be. The pattern I've described of a Supreme Court working hand-in-glove with a dominant and resilient political regime arises from the politics of such a regime. That kind of regime has basic commitments to a vision of what our nation's policies should be. Presidents choose Supreme Court justices whom, they believe, share those commitments. And, when a regime is dominant and resilient, presidents are likely to be pretty good at assessing the beliefs of those they nominate.

It's important here to emphasize that nothing in what I've said so far assumes that justices actually think about politics or how what they're doing helps or hurts the presidents who appointed them. That occasionally happens. In the early 1960s the Supreme Court was considering some cases arising out of sit-ins aimed at desegregating southern restaurants and stores. Under existing doctrine it was difficult for the Court's liberals to explain why the protestors couldn't be convicted of various law violations. For a while they managed to eke out majorities for narrow theories overturning convictions. By 1963 and 1964, though, the liberals had run out of dodges, and the Court turned to examining the central doctrinal problems. When the tentative votes were cast, it looked as if the protestors were going to lose. Justice William Brennan maneuvered rather desperately to keep the Court from handing down its decision while Congress was debating the proposed Civil Rights Act, telling his colleagues that a decision against the protestors would make it harder to get the votes in Congress for the Act.

That sort of direct attention to politics is rare. The mechanism that connects the Supreme Court to politics is indirect—and therefore imperfect. Presidents pick justices whom they believe have constitutional visions consistent with the presidents' political agendas, including the items immediately at issue in politics, such as New Deal legislation for Franklin Roosevelt, and the broader agendas that presidents seek to advance over a longer period. When things work well, the justices simply interpret the Constitution as they understand it—which is how the president wanted them to understand it. From their own point of view, that is, from the inside, the justices are entirely sincere in saying that they are doing no more than interpreting the Constitution and that they pay no attention whatever to politics. There's something to admire about a constitutional design that so seamlessly integrates law and politics —although it's not clear that a person, whether judge or ordinary citizen, who thinks that about his or her own positions can be quite as generous about the motivations of those on the other side of a constitutional dispute.

Reconstructive Presidents and Degenerating Regimes

As we've seen, not all regimes are dominant and resilient. They begin by getting a toehold, and eventually they degenerate. One thing is constant, though: Supreme Court justices have life tenure—which means that new regimes with presidents who hope to reconstruct the political order confront a Supreme Court dominated by justices appointed under the regime the president seeks to displace, and that most of the justices in place when a regime is in its last stages are holdovers from a time when that regime was young and vigorous. This is a formula for difficulties, even constitutional crises.

At this point, then, we have to modify the proposition that I used to begin this chapter. I started by saying that politicians put up with judicial review because the courts help them with some of their political tasks. I did so in order to bring out the connection between what the Supreme Court says the Constitution means and the political structures we examined in Chapter One. Now we're going to see examples of how judicial review causes problems for politicians, but the underlying goal is the same—to show the connection between political structures and the Supreme Court, so that we can understand how the Constitution as interpreted by the Supreme Court matters.

Reconstructive presidents and holdover Courts. Reconstructive presidents come into office with a policy agenda that they contend is consistent with the Constitution properly understood. When they arrive, though, the Supreme Court has been articulating a different set of constitutional understandings. That, after all, is why the president needs to "reconstruct" the constitutional order. Important parts of the president's policy agenda will be inconsistent with the constitutional principles the Court has been implementing for years, perhaps decades.

And, importantly, the president arrives alone. He has to take the Court as it is until he gets a chance—and it is a chance, an almost random event—to name new justices. The result is a high probability that the "old" Supreme Court will find unconstitutional some important parts of the "new" policy agenda.

The paradigm of the holdover Court causing a constitutional crisis is the Supreme Court in the 1930s. Republicans had controlled the national government until the Great Depression discredited their party. Republican presidents were "conservative" in the modern sense, but the Republican Party they headed was a coalition. Many Republicans took William Howard Taft, president from 1909 to 1913, as their model—and Taft was Chief Justice of the Supreme Court when the Depression hit. Others, though, took the more progressive Theodore Roosevelt as their model. As Chief Justice, Taft pushed his favored candidates on the Republican presidents of the 1920s, and had some degree of success. But his success was not complete, and when Franklin Roosevelt became president and initiated the aggressive national economic policies that we know as the New Deal, the Court was divided between four quite conservative justices, several relatively liberal justices, and a couple of moderately conservative judges who held the balance of power inside the Court.

Here the result was the constitutional crisis of 1936–37, when the Court's conservatives struck down central elements of the

New Deal and articulated constitutional doctrines that threatened the entire New Deal. Franklin Roosevelt responded by proposing to "pack the Court," expanding it so that he could appoint enough new justices to override the conservatives' objections. The Court-packing plan came within inches of success. It fell short almost certainly because the Senate's majority leader, a forceful advocate of the plan and a likely nominee to fill one of the new positions, died of a sudden heart attack probably induced by the stress of the legislative struggle in Washington's oppressively hot summer.

The crisis was resolved, though, first by what pundits of the time described as the "switch in time that saved the Nine," votes cast by Justice Owen Roberts supporting New Deal programs and seemingly inconsistent with his votes just a few months earlier, and then by a series of retirements from the Court in rapid succession.[7] The New Deal constitutional order

---

7. Today some scholars dispute the claim that Roberts changed his vote in response to external political developments such as the Court-packing plan. I am in the midst of research on this period, and my conclusions might change, but at present my view is this: Roberts certainly did not understand himself to have changed his position dramatically; developments outside the Court probably did have some subtle influence on the way Roberts interpreted the purely legal materials he had to deal with; and outside observers were not entirely wrong in their nearly unanimous view that something dramatic had happened on the Court.

came to dominate the Supreme Court, that is, through the usual mechanism of new appointees replacing old ones.

For our purposes, the important feature of the story of 1937 is its structure: Franklin Roosevelt, a reconstructive president, had to deal with a Supreme Court shaped by the regime that he proposed to transform dramatically with support from a substantial majority of the American people. Under the circumstances, a serious confrontation was inevitable, although perhaps the Court might have caved in before it was pushed—itself a form of confrontation, I think.

Reconstructive presidencies are rare, and our most recent one, Ronald Reagan's, did not provoke a constitutional crisis—which should caution against treating the scheme I'm describing as something like a mechanical "model" of how the Supreme Court matters. One reason for the difference between the effects of the New Deal Revolution and the Reagan Revolution on relations between the Supreme Court and the president is that the New Deal/Great Society order degenerated gradually, and while it did Richard Nixon was able to place relatively conservative justices on the Supreme Court. When Reagan took over, the Court had already been changed quite a bit. Another reason is that the Reagan Revolution was never a complete repudiation of the New Deal and the Great Society. Congress did not enact statutes that were dramatically inconsistent with prior constitutional understandings because Democrats controlled one or both houses of Congress through much of the period between Reagan's election and the early years of the present century. And, finally and probably most important, the Republican Party only gradually became ideologically homogeneous. Republican nominees were all relatively conservative, but some— William Rehnquist and Antonin Scalia for example—were consistently and strongly conservative, while others, such as Sandra Day O'Connor and Anthony Kennedy, were more moderate "country club Republicans." Only during George W. Bush's presidency were Supreme Court nominations the product of an ideologically homogeneous Republican Party, and not surprisingly the nominees were two strong conservatives. The Court during the Reagan era drifted to the right, more quickly than Congress or even the presidency did. But "drift" is not something that produces constitutional confrontation.

One final, quite speculative comment: There's some chance that Barack Obama will be a reconstructive president. If so, he will face a Supreme Court dominated by quite conservative justices. And those justices are relatively young. Should President Obama serve two terms, he would leave office in early 2017, when the oldest strong conservative on the Court could be Antonin Scalia, who at eighty years old would be younger than Justice John Paul Stevens is in 2010. We might find ourselves facing a new version of the New Deal confrontation between Franklin Roosevelt and the Supreme Court.

Degenerating regimes and out-of-touch Courts. As we've seen, in its heyday the Warren Court collaborated with the president and Congress in implementing the constitutional commitments of the New Deal and Great Society such as nationalism and civil rights for African Americans. By the late 1960s that constitutional regime was on its last legs, but the Warren Court kept on going. Rather than helping sustain a resilient order, the Warren Court's decisions contributed to the weakening of a declining one. Republican critics of Lyndon Johnson focused on domestic disorder—street crime, protests, some of them violent, against the war in Vietnam and against conditions in urban African American communities. They attributed that disorder to Warren Court decisions. For Republicans, and for increasing numbers of voters, holdings in favor of criminal defendants, such as the celebrated and reviled Miranda decision, emboldened criminal predators, and decisions upholding the free speech rights of political protestors left protestors free to roam the streets and cause trouble.

The Warren Court's decisions were causing President Johnson political problems that he would have liked to avoid. If he could have gotten on the phone and talked to the Warren Court's liberals, he almost certainly would have asked them to tone things down, at least a bit.[8] Some scholars have discerned a modest retreat by the Warren Court at the end of the 1960s from its expansive interpretations of the Constitution's provisions dealing with criminal procedure. I disagree,[9] but no matter how one interprets the Court's actions, they clearly weren't substantial enough to make Johnson's political life easier. Had Johnson made the phone calls, his friends on the Court would have been polite but unresponsive.

The reason arises out of the very mechanisms that connect politics and the Supreme Court. Presidents appoint justices whose overall views about the Constitution are consonant with the presidents' on the issues the president cares most about. The justices then implement their constitutional views. Most of the time presidents are fine with that. The justices' decisions, though, rest on their views about the Constitution, not on the decisions' political implications. The Warren Court's criminal procedure decisions were intimately intertwined with

8. He did talk to his friend and former lawyer Justice Abe Fortas, whom he had appointed to the Supreme Court, but the conversations were mostly about policy matters such as the conduct of the war in Vietnam.

9. In my view the decisions described as modest retreats are better described as implementing a component of Warren Court liberalism that could come to the surface only after a lot of preliminary work had been done. That component encouraged judicial deference to truly professional police judgments.

its civil rights agenda. For the Warren Court's liberals, African Americans were the primary victims of the police and prosecution practices they attacked as unconstitutional. That connection didn't disappear merely because the political environment changed.

Once again, the example illustrates a deeper structural point. Presidents serve for fixed terms, and the constitutional regimes they put in place have a life cycle. Justices serve until they decide to retire (or, occasionally, until they die with their boots on). Appointed to promote a constitutional vision, the justices do so without much regard for the immediate political consequences of their actions. A Court in sync with a president and a constitutional regime today will eventually go out of sync. With reconstructive presidents in office, that failure of synchronization can produce a constitutional confrontation, resolved typically when the president outlasts his opponents on the Court. A president in a declining political regime can only watch as the disaster unfolds.

Using the Courts to Solve Political Problems

I've used the example of courts collaborating with resilient political regimes to motivate a larger discussion of the way in which politics matters for constitutional law. Scholars have suggested another form of collaboration, about which I'm more skeptical, but discussing it does open up some new perspectives on the connection between politics and constitutional law.

I'll begin with a general and abstract description and then provide examples. Suppose you're the leader of a political party that's a coalition, and at the moment two important factions disagree, pretty strenuously, about an issue that's important to them. They are pressing you to do something on the issue, but what you do to satisfy one faction will almost certainly alienate the other. You can solve your immediate political problem, and hold your party together, by foisting the issue off on someone else. If they solve the problem, you're home free, and if they fail you can blame them. And, at the least, you can postpone your problem by kicking the can down the road. Delay might eliminate the issue from politics. You might be able to figure out some novel strategy to deal with the issue—perhaps by coming up with some other policy question on which party members are unified and that you can persuade them is vastly more important than the one they've divided over. Delay might make the problem of holding your party together someone else's problem. The Supreme Court's one of the institutions you can pass the issue off to, at least if you can give the issue a constitutional spin.

Historically, something pretty much fitting that description occurred on the issue of the constitutionality of congressional regulation of slavery in the nation's western territories. By the middle of the 1850s that had become the focal point of the national controversy over slavery. The Democratic Party was divided between southerners committed to slavery and its extension, and northern "doughfaces," as they were called, who were willing to leave slavery untouched in the South but were uncomfortable with extending it to the territories of Kansas and Nebraska. Leaders of the national party discovered a lawsuit that could be used to raise the issue of Congress's power to regulate slavery in the territories. They hoped that the Supreme Court could resolve the issue, allowing the party's leaders to hold the party together without requiring that the party take a position on the issue. Before the Supreme Court handed down its decision, President James Buchanan learned what it planned to do and used his inaugural address in 1857 to urge all Americans to accept the Court's impending decision and, as we would now say, move on.

The issue of abortion had a similar structure when it came to the fore in the late 1960s. Abortion was difficult for Democratic politicians because their party was a coalition including both urban whites of Irish, Italian, and Polish origin, many of whom were Catholics who opposed making access to abortions easier, and cosmopolitan liberals who favored easing restrictions on the availability of abortion. The law-and-order issue was already alienating urban ethnics from the party, and its leaders didn't need more trouble. Republican leaders faced a similar political problem over the abortion issue. Their party was a coalition too. Its northeastern wing was relatively liberal on social issues; indeed, in 1970 Nelson Rockefeller had promoted and signed a law essentially eliminating New York's restrictions on the availability of abortion.[10] The party's southern strategy, promoted by Barry Goldwater and Richard Nixon, was in its early stages, but the party could not afford to undermine that strategy by endorsing socially liberal positions. Getting the Supreme Court to "resolve" the abortion issue might solve the problems faced within both parties of keeping their coalitions together.

As we know, the strategy of deferring issues that divide party coalitions to the Supreme Court didn't work for slavery or for abortion. The Supreme Court denied Congress the power to regulate slavery in the territories in the *Dred Scott* decision, Republican Abraham Lincoln won the presidency three years later, the South seceded, and the Civil War ensued. The Supreme Court severely restricted states' ability to restrict the availability of abortions in *Roe v. Wade,* and the abortion issue became a central issue in elections thereafter.

The reasons for these failures are important, because they bring out another aspect of the structure of constitutional

10. California's governor Ronald Reagan also signed a "liberal" abortion bill, which indicates the strength of abortion liberals within the Republican Party in the late 1960s.

politics. Political leaders might hope that a Supreme Court decision could indeed take a divisive issue out of politics. And it might, if enough party members are willing to subordinate their own views about the policy issue to the Supreme Court's constitutional decision. They have to say, "Well, I care about preventing slavery from extending to the territories, but now that the Supreme Court's told me that the Constitution bars me from getting that policy, I guess I'll just move on." That can happen if the issue doesn't matter all that much to the voter. The problem political leaders face, though, is precisely that the issue they've passed off to the Court is one that party members care a lot about. So, in general, the strategy of passing issues off to the Court won't take the issue out of politics. (It will delay resolution of the issue, which might be enough for some party leaders.)

What happens politically when the Court comes down on one side of these issues that divide party coalitions? Party leaders hope to be able to say to the winning side that they don't have to press the politicians to do anything because the Court's given the winners what they want, and to say to the losers that the politicians would like to help them but unfortunately can't do anything about what the Court has done. The message to the winners is likely to get through, but not so the message to the losers. They can respond that there is indeed something the politicians can do—test the limits of the Court's decision, and eventually appoint new and better justices. That was Abraham Lincoln's strategy after *Dred Scott*, which he said he accepted as a decision in that particular case but would not accept as what he called a "rule of political action," one that would prevent Republicans from pursuing other lines of attack on slavery. It was the strategy of the pro-life movement after *Roe v. Wade* as well.

Supreme Court decisions on these kinds of issues—those that divide political coalitions—lead party factions to rebalance their portfolios, in modern financial jargon. Before the Court's decision, the factions invest some of their energy in legal action, and some in political action. After the Court's decision, the losers shift resources from law to politics because they know they can't accomplish anything in the short run through lawsuits—and, importantly, the winners shift resources from politics to law, relying on the courts to bail them out if they lose in politics. These strategies make sense for both sides in the short run, but they lead to long-run problems for the apparent winners. Eventually the latter figure this out, but by then they are playing catch-up, which isn't a good strategy in politics.

To sum up this section: Politics provides some incentives for politicians to try to use the Supreme Court to address the politicians' political problems. The Court's actions matter in the short run because they do something, one way or the other, about a policy issue that the politicians haven't been able to address. They matter in the long run because of their effects on politics.

How Politics Affects Constitutional Ideas

It won't have escaped your notice that I've said a lot about why and how politics matters for the Constitution, and not much at all about why and how ideas about what the Constitution means matter. Constitutional ideas do matter, but not in the way you might think. During his confirmation hearings Clarence Thomas said that he would approach constitutional questions "stripped down like a runner," without ideological presuppositions. Most legal academics regarded that as silly, as they did Sonia Sotomayor's assertions that she would simply apply the law to the facts. Supreme Court justices are appointed in part because of the general views they have about what the Constitution means, and once on the Court they interpret the Constitution according to those views.

The constitutional views a justice has are typically a combination of some quite specific propositions with some relatively abstract ideas and some ideas about how the justice is supposed to go about interpreting the Constitution. For example, today's conservative judges tend to believe that the Constitution does not protect a right to choose with respect to abortion, that the Constitution cautions against letting the national government exercise too much power, and, more or less, that original understandings of constitutional terms matter a great deal (unless those understandings conflict with the specific or the abstract ideas to which contemporary conservatives are committed). Today's liberal judges obviously have a different package of beliefs.

These packages are the judicial version of the ideas associated with the core of the policies that characterize the position of the president who appointed individual judges. And, again, those policies are themselves related to the president's position with respect to political time—the regime he is affiliated with or seeking to reconstruct, for example. So, in the large, politics affects constitutional ideas through presidential elections and judicial nominations. No news here. The fact that judges have packages of constitutional ideas opens new issues, though. Two characteristics of these packages are particularly important.

- *Loose connections.* The elements in the packages are only loosely connected. There's no strongly logical connection between thinking that the national government should be reasonably small and thinking that there's no constitutional right to choose with respect to abortion. The judge's job is to figure out how one or another element applies in a specific case, and then how that application fits into the entire package. It would be awkward for contemporary conservative jurists to hold that the Constitution required that states have quite restrictive abortion laws, for example, because that would put the "small national government" view in tension with the "no right to choose" view, unless they managed to banish from their minds the attacks they themselves have leveled against the Supreme Court as an instrument of a "big" national government when it does things they don't like.[11]

· *Times and issues change (once again).* Constitutional issues change over time—or at least, old problems present themselves in a new guise. Judges then have to figure out how their old ideas apply to the new problems and, again, how those new applications fit into their overall visions of the Constitution.

Consider here racial equality in two constitutional regimes, the New Deal order and the Reagan Revolution. As I've noted, racial equality wasn't an important part of the New Deal's

11. The loose connections mean that long-term visions of the Constitution or short-term political considerations can dictate how the judge resolves a specific case, but they also mean that the judge will ordinarily be able to make sense of his or her constitutional work as a whole.

core. Economic equality was.[12] Not equality in form, though—equality in substance. For New Dealers the government had the power to address situations in which the distribution of economic and political power put some people in subordinate positions that couldn't easily be justified. Labor unions were central to the Democratic Party coalition, the rights of labor central to the New Deal's principles.

Upholding minimum wage legislation in 1937, for example, Chief Justice Charles Evans Hughes wrote that the "community is not bound to provide what is in effect a subsidy for unconscionable employers." Low wages were a subsidy "in effect" because they benefited employers at the expense of their workers, which was inconsistent with New Deal ideas about economic equality. The "community" could intervene to eliminate the subsidy by legislating a minimum wage. The New Deal concern for subordination went beyond economics—and legislation. Eleven months after the minimum wage decision, Justice Harlan Fiske Stone wrote what has been called the most famous footnote in Supreme Court history. For our purposes, the key passage in what's known as "Footnote Four" is this: "Nor need we enquire . . . whether prejudice against discrete

12. Provisions on the New Deal's minimum wage legislation exempting agricultural and household workers from its requirements demonstrate the priority of economics over race in the New Deal.

and insular minorities may be a special condition, which tends seriously to curtail the operation of those political processes ordinarily to be relied upon to protect minorities, and which may call for a correspondingly more searching judicial inquiry." Footnote Four makes analysis of how politics actually operates central to the Constitution's promotion of equality in the New Deal vision.

Understanding equality in effect to be a core New Deal commitment, New Deal justices were pushed in the direction of finding racial segregation unconstitutional. Indeed, the push was so strong that when the justices focused on politics as they discussed *Brown v. Board of Education,* their conversation concerned not why it made political sense to find segregation unconstitutional but what political obstacles there might be if they did so.

What ideal of equality did the New Deal Court articulate in *Brown?* The 1954 decision and its follow-up a year later dealing with the remedy for unconstitutional segregation, which used the famous phrase "all deliberate speed," combined themes of formal equality and equality in effect—desegregation and integration as distinct policies—but formal equality pretty clearly played a subordinate role. Southern resistance to desegregation encouraged the justices to think more about equality, and made integration an increasingly attractive version of racial equality for the justices. Affirmative action took hold as a serious national policy in the early 1960s, and it too fit into a version of equality focused on effects. In the 1930s and 1940s New Dealers knew about and opposed the use of quotas in employment and education; their mental image of such quotas were restrictions on Jewish employment and admission to elite universities, but they saw the same threat when African Americans promoted boycotts under the slogan "Don't Buy Where You Can't Work." By the 1960s the inheritors of the New Deal's legacy believed that racial equality meant equality in effect, and so believed that voluntary affirmative action programs were clearly constitutional. When the Burger Court considered the use of busing to remedy the persisting effects of prior segregation in the public schools, the idea that substantive equality mattered more than formal equality was so deeply embedded that the issue the Court dealt with was whether courts could order school boards to take the racial composition of schools into account when they assigned students to schools; it almost literally went without saying that school boards could voluntarily take race into account to achieve integrated outcomes.

By the 1960s, then, the New Deal's commitment to equality in effect had spread broadly into constitutional law. Then came the Reagan Revolution. The Republicans' southern strategy capitalized on opposition to desegregation and, even more, on opposition in the North as well as the South to busing as a remedy for segregation. The Republican vision of constitutional equality was formal, as expressed in the only dissent from the 1896 Supreme Court decision upholding a segregation law. There Justice John Marshall Harlan wrote, "The Constitution is color-blind." For the Reagan Revolution, this meant that segregation statutes were unconstitutional because they made race relevant to public policy. That explained why affirmative action was unconstitutional too. And, by 2007, it explained the unconstitutionality of policies adopted by school boards that thought it good social policy to have integrated schools and classrooms and then sought to achieve that goal by assigning students to schools with some attention to their race.

Equality was central to the New Deal's concerns, but not racial equality. As New Deal justices thought about equality and what the New Deal's commitments to equality were, they came to see implications of those commitments for racial equality. Changes in the political environment affected how the justices thought about racial equality, of course, but we shouldn't try to disentangle politics and ideas. Both mattered. By the 1960s and 1970s the regime commitments of the New Deal/Great Society order were quite different from what they had been a few decades earlier. The Reagan Revolution was more directly committed to a particular vision of racial equality, and its justices implemented that vision without much change over their careers.[13]

Social Movements and Constitutional Understandings

I've described the way in which the principles animating different constitutional regimes develop over time. I've emphasized that some of what the justices do is simply work out the implications, as they see them, of the more abstract of the principles within a loose package. I've also suggested, though, that the political environment matters for what the justices think their principles mean. I want to stress the latter phrase—for what the justices think their principles mean—and deal with some implications. It's not just that the justices operate within a political context, doing things that help or hinder their political allies. In addition, the world in which the justices live affects what they think the Constitution means—

13. My personal view, supported by snippets of data but no more than that, is that in the mid-and late 1970s Warren Burger and William Rehnquist, conservative Republican appointees to the Supreme Court before the Reagan Revolution, would have been surprised at claims that the Constitution prohibited school boards from achieving integrated schools and classrooms by paying attention to students' race, because the Reagan Revolution's regime commitment to formal equality had not fully taken hold among conservatives.

and as the world changes, so can their understandings of the Constitution.

Probably the best modern example of what I'm concerned with here is the constitutional status of gay and lesbian rights. Until the 1970s, the idea that the Constitution protected gays and lesbians as such, that is, on the basis of their sexual orientation, would have been laughable. As Justice Byron White put it as late as 1986, the claim that there was a constitutional right to homosexual sodomy deeply rooted in the nation's tradition was, he thought, "facetious." Only a handful of Supreme Court justices took any gay rights claims seriously until the 1980s, and no Supreme Court majority did until the mid-1990s. Then things changed. In 1996 the Court held unconstitutional a Colorado initiative that purported to exclude gays and lesbians from the coverage of any state antidiscrimination law, and in 2003 it invalidated the relatively small number of state statutes still making sodomy a crime.

Both these decisions might be handled under the heading "outliers." No state had a measure as extreme as Colorado's in its denial of protection to gays and lesbians, and by the time the Court decided the sodomy case it noted that only twelve states had similar laws on the books, and the trend throughout the nation had clearly been in the direction of protecting gay and lesbian rights. Yet, there's a difference between these cases and the "outlier" cases I discussed earlier. The latter cases were ones in which the Supreme Court was doing work that politicians in a resilient constitutional regime didn't have time to do themselves. The Reagan Revolution had a libertarian strand, but no one seriously thinks that Reagan Republicans around the turn of the twenty-first century wanted to get rid of sodomy laws but simply couldn't get around to doing so. And, of course, no justice was appointed to the Supreme Court because of his or her views about gay and lesbian rights.

Maybe the entire explanation for the emergence of a constitutional law protecting gay and lesbian rights is happenstance: Justice Lewis Powell, a traditionalist conservative, retired and was replaced by Anthony Kennedy, a conservative with some libertarian leanings. But the story of women's rights is similar— a dramatic change in constitutional law without a large enough change in the Court's composition to explain the doctrinal change. Here's a general version of what happened with women's rights and, to a lesser extent, with gay and lesbian rights. The Constitution as interpreted by the Supreme Court changed without any relevant change in the Court's composition.[14] That

14. The story of women's rights is made a bit more complicated because Justice Ruth Bader Ginsburg was appointed to the Court in part because of her activism on behalf of women's rights, and because Justice Sandra Day O'Connor was appointed primarily because Ronald Reagan had made a campaign promise to appoint a woman to the Supreme Court. Most though not all of the doctrinal changes re-

has to be something of a puzzle for the approach I've developed so far, where the driver that determines how the Constitution matters is politics operating through Supreme Court appointments. Obviously, in this setting some justices have changed their minds. What we need is some way of understanding why that happens.

New experiences. One common suggestion is that justices change their minds about what the Constitution means because they have new experiences. The most prominent examples offered from recent history involve Justice Lewis Powell and Chief Justice William Rehnquist.

Justice Powell found *Bowers v. Hardwick,* the Court's 1987 sodomy case, quite difficult. He went back and forth over whether to find prohibitions on homosexual sodomy unconstitutional or to uphold them. Eventually he voted to uphold them, observing tepidly that he might have come out differently if the case had involved a defendant who had been sentenced to a long prison sentence for the offense. While he was still up in the air about what to do, within his chambers he observed to the law clerk handling the case that he had never known a homosexual. The law clerk, himself gay, refrained

---

garding women's constitutional rights had occurred before Justices O'Connor and Ginsburg arrived at the Court, but their presence and the politics associated with their appointments make the story about gay and lesbian rights a bit more illuminating for my argument.

from disabusing the justice. It's a common view that Powell might have cast his vote differently had he been aware that he had known and worked closely with gays.

In his first years on the Court Justice Rehnquist regularly voted against claims that women were denied their constitutional right to equal treatment by laws that treated them categorically differently from men. Near the end of his tenure, though, his position seemed to have changed. He agreed that Virginia's law barring women from attending the Virginia Military Institute was unconstitutional, for example, and he wrote the Court's opinion rejecting a constitutional challenge to the federal Family and Parental Leave Act, writing an opinion that described as discriminatory social practices resting on the assumption that women more often than men would have the responsibility for taking care of sick children. Some observers explain his later votes by referring to the Chief Justice's observation of the difficulties faced by his daughter, a single mother pursuing a career as a lawyer.

I personally wouldn't make too much of these examples, or of the broader idea that new experience leads individual justices to change the minds about what the Constitution means. The examples are highly speculative, resting on no direct evidence. The story about Justice Powell is explicitly counterfactual in its assumption that he would have acted differently had he known what he didn't know.[15] The story about Chief Justice Rehnquist doesn't take into account that precedent had been accumulating by the time he cast his later votes, and deference to established law might explain the apparent change in his constitutional views.

Against the idea that new experiences help change minds is the fact that Supreme Court justices aren't spring chickens. They've already had a lot of experiences, undoubtedly the kinds that had shaped their understanding of the Constitution's meaning. Give them a new experience, though, and the chances are they'll ignore it or explain it away within the framework they've already established for themselves.

Social movements. It's no accident that the best examples of constitutional doctrine changing without relevant changes in the Court's composition involve gay and lesbian rights and women's rights. When a lot of people start acting up—sometimes within the framework of party politics, more often outside it, as what the framers' generation called "the people out of doors"—political elites take notice. Party politicians start to ask themselves whether they can adjust their party platforms to draw some of these newly active citizens into their party and

15. After his retirement—and after his position in *Bowers* had been widely criticized—Justice Powell did say that he (then) thought that his vote had been a mistake. That's not quite direct evidence supporting the counterfactual view, but it deserves mention.

keep them away from their opponents'. The accommodations won't betray their party's fundamental principles, but they will try to appropriate elements of the social movement's concerns and fit those elements within the party's overall approach to public policy. Party leaders who figure this out may find themselves in control of the presidency, at which point they will think about the political benefits of choosing justices who will see the social movement's principles in the Constitution.

Importantly, judges do something quite similar, but with ideas as their only tools, not appointments. The very existence of a social movement tells judges that a lot of people think that what they are asking for is required by the American political ethos—freedom of expression, gender equality, or whatever the social movement's concerns are. Whatever the regime principles to which an individual justice is committed, concerns like those are likely to be present at least on the abstract level. Action by the people out of doors can prod a judge into thinking through exactly what those abstract principles mean. Adjustment isn't always going to happen. The judge may end up thinking that the social movement is just wrong about what equality entails, for example. Or the movement's demands can't be fit comfortably within the judge's overall conceptual framework. Sometimes, though, the judge will conclude that the social movement's constitutional vision is admirably consistent with the regime principles to which the judge is committed—and the judge will find in the Constitution a doctrine that he wouldn't have found there before the social movement went into the streets.

The social movement story about women's rights is reasonably straightforward. The New Deal and Great Society justices were committed to ideas about equality and the elimination of subordination. The women's movement of the 1960s and 1970s offered its own version of ideas about equality, which were compatible with the New Deal/Great Society ideas. The New Deal and Great Society justices moved seamlessly to incorporate women's equality into the overall constitutional framework to which they were committed. The justices of the Reagan Revolution (and its Nixonian precursor) could follow a similarly smooth course with respect to claims for formal equality by women. They adopted the principle of formal equality to deal with race discrimination, where it meant that governments could not rely on race as a reason for acting. When the modern women's movement appeared, these justices could move, again seamlessly, to the principle of formal gender equality, the proposition that governments could not rely on gender as a reason for acting. Formal equality wouldn't satisfy all the demands articulated by leaders of the modern women's movement, but it was good enough to propel the constitutionalization of gender equality.

Add liberty or autonomy to equality in the context of the movement for gay and lesbian rights, and you have a pretty good story about why the Supreme Court switched from being gay-hostile to being reasonably gay-friendly. Again, the gay and lesbian social movement hasn't gotten everything it wants from the Supreme Court (yet). It surely has gotten more over the past decade than gays and lesbians had throughout the Court's history.

Paying attention to social movements helps us complete the story I started to outline about abortion rights. Here too we need to pay attention to the regime principles of the New Deal and the Great Society. When Arthur Goldberg joined the Supreme Court in 1962 it finally had a solid bloc of unambiguous and unambivalent liberals, no longer worried about the charge leveled by earlier New Deal justices against the pre-1937 Court that judicial activism was bad no matter whose interests activism served. They looked around American society and saw "sex, drugs, and rock 'n' roll," and weren't all that disturbed. Perhaps it's not accurate to call what happened in the 1960s a social movement, but certainly the people were acting out of doors in ways that had clear political import. The justices understood that some of their earlier decisions, such as those making it more difficult for governments to prohibit the distribution of sexually explicit material, had contributed to what they were seeing. The activism of the 1960s prodded the Court's liberals to think through the principles to which they were committed. They discovered that decisions like *Griswold v. Connecticut*, which I discussed under the heading of "outliers," made sense if they incorporated a principle of individual autonomy into the package of principles to which they were committed. And, on further reflection, they discovered that the real foundation of their earlier commitments to racial equality and freedom of expression was exactly the same principle of autonomy. Then, when they faced the abortion issue, they had a regime principle in hand that directed a resolution.

So far the examples I've used have involved social movements on the liberal side of the political spectrum. There are conservative social movements too, such as the Christian Right. As with other social movements, the primary effects of modern conservative social movements have been on judicial appointments. We have to look carefully to see the effects of those movements on the ideas of judges not themselves appointed as a result of the movements' incorporation in the modern Republican Party. A good starting point is this. The Christian Right has transformed the law of church-state relations—again, mostly through the appointment mechanism. The Supreme Court doctrine that attracted the most fire from the Christian Right is probably the "*Lemon* test," named for the decision that set out the doctrine. Notably, that decision was written by Warren Burger, a conservative Republican from the era before the Christian Right was fully incorporated into the Republican Party.

The Christian Right's effect as a social movement can be seen in how the Court's liberals have started to approach issues of religious liberty and nonestablishment. The core constitutional commitments of the New Deal and the Great Society were deeply secularist, seeing no substantial role for religious institutions to play in public life.[16] With the rise of the Christian Right, liberal formulations of the principle barring establishments of religion have struggled to disclaim the secularism to which earlier generations of liberals were committed. The Court's liberals regularly cast their votes against practices that intertwine religion and public policy too directly, but their opinions are full of statements asserting their respect for religion and its important place in public life. As with Chief Justice Rehnquist's late opinions on women's rights, here too the liberals may be acknowledging the force of accumulated precedent. They may also be reflecting the effect of the Christian Right as a social movement on their own understanding of the Constitution.

Conclusion

So: To understand how the Supreme Court matters, pay attention to what kind of president we have (reconstructive, affiliated,

---

16. As John Jeffries and James Ryan have shown, there was a strand of anti-Catholicism in this.

preemptive), whether the president is part of a constitutional regime that is resilient or declining, how long the justices on the Supreme Court have been there and who appointed them, whether the national government is divided or unified, whether (or the degree to which) our political parties are coalitions of disparate groups or are ideologically homogeneous, and whether there's some social movement that seems important even though it hasn't yet achieved real electoral success. Once you do that, you'll have about as good a sense of what fundamental rights the Supreme Court is going to enforce as any scholar who specializes in studying the Constitution and the Court. You won't get everything right. No one does. There are too many moving parts to get right. Each of the nine justices will have a different take on a particular case and its political environment, and even slight differences, when multiplied by three, four, or even nine, can make a large difference in outcome. Still, you'll understand the main trends in the Court's decisions—and you won't have to worry too much about the details of the constitutional doctrines that drive the Court's decisions from the inside.

3

how

to

make

the

constitution

matter

more—

or

differently

Some may find my argument disquieting, and not simply because it deemphasizes the "fundamental rights" answer to the question of whether the Constitution matters in favor of an account in which the Constitution matters because it creates and structures our politics. I believe that bringing politics to the fore will actually improve the constitutional discussions we have when we talk about a recent Supreme Court decision or consider a nomination to the Supreme Court. And, because the structure the Constitution creates for our politics is rather loose, we can work around its restrictive provisions if we want to—and in doing so actually respect our constitutional heritage.

Why "Fundamental Rights" Aren't Enough

Consider the implications of the "fundamental rights" answer. As I've repeatedly emphasized, people disagree about what fundamental rights we have. In reaffirming what it called the "central holding" of *Roe v. Wade,* three Justices of the Supreme Court foolishly contended that the Court's role was to settle deep disagreements about our fundamental rights: "Where, in the performance of its judicial duties, the Court decides a case in such a way as to resolve the sort of intensely divisive controversy reflected in *Roe* and those rare, comparable cases, its decision has a dimension that the resolution of the normal case does not carry. It is the dimension present whenever the Court's interpretation of the Constitution calls the contending sides of a national controversy to end their national division by accepting a common mandate rooted in the Constitution."

The Court's failure to "end" the "national division" over whether the Constitution protects a fundamental right to choose was surely inevitable. And the failure was probably a good thing too. How can we deal with deep and persisting disagreement about what our fundamental rights are? By coming to grips with the fact that these disagreements are reasonable, no different in principle from our disagreements about how to finance a national health care policy or about the proper tax rate for capital gains.

Suppose the Supreme Court divides five to four on some question about fundamental rights that you care about a lot. If you think that the Constitution matters because it protects our fundamental rights, what are you going to think about the justices who disagreed with you? You have considered what the Constitution means, and you've come up with your answer. Anyone who disagrees with you must be a fool or a knave—a fool, unable to perform the task of constitutional interpretation with sufficient care and attention, or a knave, willfully disregarding the "true" Constitution in pursuit of a personal or partisan agenda. And, because we're dealing here with deep and persistent disagreements, it doesn't matter whether the knaves and fools number four, when you've won your case, or five, when you've lost. Something has to account for their blindness, no matter their numbers or the formal authority that comes from having five votes on the Supreme Court.

This is not a formula for an elevated discussion about the Constitution's meaning, or even for a decent conversation about what our fundamental rights really are. My complicated description of perceiving the Court's decisions about fundamental rights as arising out of politics allows us to treat our disagreements about fundamental rights as political too. We know that in ordinary politics we're going to win some votes on important matters, and lose others. We know how to deal with our defeats and with the fact that there seem to be a fair number of people who disagree with us. We could hope that treating constitutional politics in the same way would improve our political discussions overall.

This is only a hope, though. My experience in teaching constitutional law from the perspective I've presented here is not, to be frank, all that encouraging. My students will generally nod in agreement when I describe disagreements about what our fundamental rights are as reasonable—as long as I make the statements completely abstract.[1] But describe as reasonable the disagreement between those who think there's a right to choice with respect to abortion and those who think there's a right to life, and the superficial agreement with the abstract proposition disappears. I think that's unfortunate, but I'm afraid that I haven't figured out how to help my students appreciate why treating constitutional interpretation as a form of politics is actually good for us.

1. Unless I raise the question on an examination, in which case all but my best students are shrewd enough to parrot back to me the positions I've taken in class.

Dealing With Defeat

Suppose, though, that we've managed to get enough of our fellow citizens to agree that the Constitution matters because of the way it structures our politics, and that the fundamental rights the Supreme Court says we have are guaranteed by the operation of politics within that structure. And suppose that you find yourself on the losing side too often. You might conclude that you simply have to figure out a more effective set of political strategies. There's another possibility, though. You might end up thinking that you're losing so often because our political structure is stacked against you.

That's the conclusion suggested by some important recent books criticizing the "hard-wired" features of our constitutional system. Political scientist Larry Sabato offers twenty-three "proposals to revitalize Constitution," law professor Sanford Levinson about a dozen. It's worth considering the substance of some of their proposals, and the processes available to implement them. My bottom line is that if we care enough about the proposals to implement them through the constitutional amendment process advocated by Sabato and Levinson, we can implement them through legislation.

Changing the Hard-wired Constitution: Substance

Sabato and Levinson propose more then twenty reforms, and it would be unnecessarily tedious to work through them all.[2] Some could be adopted with no changes in the written Constitution. Sabato urges that congressional districting be done by nonpartisan commissions. Congress could mandate that procedure by exercising its power to "prescribe" the "Manner of holding Elections," just as it has required that states use single districts for House elections. Or, to make an important point for my overall argument, at least there's a substantial argument supporting that proposition. Constitutional objections would probably fade away if a political movement had enough clout to get such a statute enacted, although we would have to worry that a holdover Supreme Court might invalidate it until the Court itself was transformed by the political movement that got the statute enacted. Levinson wants to eliminate "lame duck" congressional sessions, particularly where an election has substantially changed the partisan makeup of one or both houses. This too could be accomplished by statute.[3]

2. I'm going to assume that the proposals make sense as policy so that I can focus on their constitutional dimensions.

3. Indeed, a statute's almost certainly a better way to do it than a constitutional amendment, because a statute is more likely than an amendment to include a trigger allowing postelection sessions if

There are pretty good close substitutes for other reform proposals. Sabato suggests that we could take advantage of the accumulated experience of our chief executives by giving them "at large" seats in the Senate.[4] Instead, we might create a permanent commission with former presidents and vice-presidents as members, and authorize or even require it to make recommendations to the Senate on important legislative proposals. Some proposals simply require that Congress exercise the power it already has. Sabato wants to limit presidential power over war initiation. A Congress that is determined enough to limit the president can do so by exercising its power to control the Defense Department budget. A public that is determined enough to force through a constitutional amendment limiting presidential power ought to have enough influence on its representatives to get them to limit presidential power without a constitutional amendment.

---

the partisan composition hasn't changed a lot, or in emergencies, and the like.

4. John Quincy Adams served in the House of Representatives after completing his term as president. More recently, former vice president Walter Mondale ran unsuccessfully for a Senate seat, when he was placed on the ballot after Senator Paul Wellstone's death in an airplane crash shortly before election day.

Constitutional Workarounds

Another possibility is using what I've called a constitutional workaround. Something that specialists call the "Saxbe fix" illustrates how constitutional workarounds operate. The Constitution's Emoluments Clause provides, "No Senator . . . shall, during the Time for which he was elected, be appointed to any civil Office under the Authority of the United States, . . . the Emoluments whereof shall have been encreased during such time." On the face of it, the Emoluments Clause means that if Congress increases the salaries of cabinet members in 2003, a senator elected in 2000 can't take a cabinet post until her term expires in 2007. The Emoluments Clause resulted from a combination of concerns—about the possibility that the president would corrupt members of Congress by getting them to trade their votes for the prospect of appointment to a newly lucrative position, and about the possibility that members of Congress would find it to their advantage to expand the national government's size by creating positions they themselves could fill. Even if you think that these risks remain important, it's pretty clear that today the Emoluments Clause is a feeble constraint on corruption and government expansion. And it does have some costs, denying the president the chance to appoint to the cabinet people who might be the best qualified overall for positions there.

The Saxbe fix is the way we've come to work around the Emoluments Clause. Although the Saxbe fix goes back to the nineteenth century, it got its name when President Richard Nixon needed to appoint an attorney general to restore a semblance of regularity at the Department of Justice after the Saturday Night Massacre. Ford believed that William Saxbe, then a senator, could restore congressional and public trust in that department. The problem was that the attorney general's salary had indeed "been encreased" during Saxbe's term as senator. No problem, though. Congress quickly passed a statute reducing the attorney general's salary back to the same level it was before Saxbe became a senator. The idea is that the Emoluments Clause doesn't prohibit a senator from taking a cabinet post if the salary has been increased but then decreased, leaving the "net" salary the same as it had been.[5]

"No problem," though, only if you either ignore the Emoluments Clause or give it what many people think is a strained reading. The difficulty is the phrase "shall have been encreased." The natural reading of that phrase is that it refers to some action that took place in the past, not to the net salary resulting from an increase followed by a decrease. Linguists say that occasionally "shall have been" can take on what lawyers have started

5. The most recent use of the Saxbe fix occurred to allow Hillary Clinton to serve as secretary of state.

calling an "on net" meaning, and maybe they're right. Still, many people have a nagging sense that the Saxbe fix doesn't fit well with the language of the Emoluments Clause. No one cares, though. Finicky constitutionalists might object that, to adapt the title of one article on the subject, Hillary Clinton is unconstitutional, but even they don't think that using the Emoluments Clause to keep her from serving as secretary of state indicates how well-designed our Constitution is.

The Saxbe fix shows how we can work around the Emoluments Clause. Why do we use it? The answer combines policy and politics. Political elites, and probably anyone who becomes aware of the Emoluments Clause problem, don't think that the Clause does anything useful anymore. That is, they believe that it's now a bug in our constitutional system. Importantly, that belief is shared across the political spectrum.

More generally, constitutional workarounds are devices that allow us to ignore what we've come to believe are flaws in our constitutional system. They work when the belief that something is a flaw is widespread and held by large numbers of people without regard to their partisan affiliations. Workarounds also tend not to have obvious policy effects. Conservative and liberal presidents like the Saxbe fix, for example, because it gives them another tool to use in addressing political problems. Saying that workarounds don't have obvious policy effects, though, is just another way of saying that they are good-government reforms.

With this background, consider a few constitutional work-arounds.

A national popular vote for president. Suppose you thought that our method of electing the president was flawed because indirect elections using the electoral college give candidates bad incentives. Smaller states have more votes in the electoral college than their populations warrant on some theories of democracy. States' votes in the electoral college are determined by adding up the number of their representatives in the House of Representatives (a figure that's roughly proportional to population), plus two more to account for a state's senators. The latter number distorts population proportionality. Presidential candidates should, and do, spend a bit more time campaigning in smaller states because of this. More important, by tradition though not by constitutional law or national statute, every electoral vote from a state is cast for the candidate who wins a plurality of that state's overall vote.[6] This "unit rule" means that

6. As I noted in Chapter One, Nebraska and Maine allocate electoral votes to the winners in each state's house districts, with the two bonus votes going to the statewide winner. As a result, in the 2008 presidential election Barack Obama won one of Nebraska's electoral votes.

presidential candidates campaign only in battleground states and not in states where they're sure to win by a plurality because the size of the margin in the noncompetitive states doesn't matter. Yet those nonbattleground states—California, Texas, New York, and others—are important to the nation, and it probably would be a good thing if presidential candidates were to design their campaigns with an eye to the size of their winning or losing margins in those states. The unit rule creates the possibility that a candidate can become president without winning more votes than the losing candidate, a possibility that's been realized several times in our history.[7]

Suppose you thought that it would be a good idea—a fix of a bug in our Constitution's design—to ensure that the candidate who won more votes nationwide than any other became president. Maybe Congress could pass a statute abolishing the unit rule, although it would take a fair amount of creative constitutional reasoning to figure out where in the Constitution Con-

---

7. Still, it's important not to overemphasize the fact, for example, that Al Gore won more votes in the 2000 presidential election than George W. Bush did, because the candidates allocated their campaign efforts in light of the unit rule in place. Had the rule in place been that the winner of more votes overall was the winner, the candidates would have conducted their campaigns differently, and we can't know whether, for example, Bush's campaign might have narrowed his losing margin in California by enough to offset Gore's margin, whatever it might have been, in Florida.

gress got the power to do that.[8] Proponents of a national popular vote for president have developed a workaround. States set the rules for casting electoral votes. Suppose a group of states with a majority of the votes in the electoral college agreed that their electors would cast their votes for the national popular vote winner. That candidate would then get a majority of the electoral votes and would become president. The problem is getting agreement among the states. The workaround is this: Each state enacts a statute requiring its electors to cast their votes for the national popular vote winner, contingent on the adoption of the same rule by other states amounting to a majority of the votes in the electoral college.

Can the states actually get away with this? On the policy level you might worry about the willingness of California's electors to cast their votes for a Republican who won the national popular vote but lost California's popular vote by a large margin. It's an open constitutional question whether a state can "require" its electors to do anything other than exercise their best judgment about who should be president. The Constitution prohibits states from entering into "compacts" with each other without congressional consent. Maybe a state statute that takes effect only if other states do something is in effect a

8. The clause giving Congress the power to regulate the time, place, and manner of elections deals only with congressional elections.

compact that requires congressional approval. We don't need to worry about these issues, though. If the supporters of the national popular vote got enough support in enough state legislatures, the pressure to go along—call it "the Electoral College fix"—would be quite strong. The fix's supporters would press Congress to approve the fix as a compact, and perhaps a majority in Congress would go along, particularly if, as I think is true, the fix's partisan effects are unclear.

Fixed terms for Supreme Court justices. The idea that well-designed constitutions have provisions allowing independent courts to determine whether legislation is constitutional has spread from the United States throughout the world. The precise design of the U.S. Supreme Court has not. Almost every nation that has come to the design issue anew has rejected the U.S. system of life tenure for constitutional court judges, preferring relatively long fixed terms and mandatory retirement ages.[9]

Sabato and Levinson would like to change our system of life tenure. Can we work around the Constitution's express provi-

9. The judgment other systems' designers have made is that terms of between twelve and fifteen years are about right, coupled with some rules about reappointment (generally not allowed) and postretirement employment (so that judges don't make decisions with an eye to their postretirement prospects).

sion that judges "shall hold their Offices during good Behaviour"? A bipartisan group of scholars has proposed a workaround, which they believe can be adopted by statute.[10] The basic idea is that the Constitution requires that a judge serve for life as a judge, but not that he or she serve for life as a judge of a particular court. So, they say, we could create limited terms for Supreme Court justices by saying that you get nominated and confirmed to a seat on the Supreme Court, where you'll serve for eighteen years. After that you're still a federal judge, but you'll sit on a court of appeals or a district court.

Of course we can raise constitutional questions about this proposal, and some who support the idea of term limits for judges think that a constitutional amendment is required. One difficulty is that judges, in the Constitution's words, "hold . . . Offices," and presidents have the power to "nominate . . . Judges of the Supreme Court." Perhaps Supreme Court justices are nominated and confirmed for a particular office. Another is that two hundred years of tradition have to count for something. Again, though, the merits of these constitutional objections aren't our concern here. The political perspective on the Constitution I've developed in this book once again

10. I should note that I agree with the proposal and agree that it can be adopted by statute. For contingent reasons I have not signed on to the most recent version of the proposal.

suggests that constitutional workarounds work—become re-garded as constitutionally permissible—when there's enough political support for them. "Enough" means "a lot," but less than you'd need to amend the Constitution.

Impossible workarounds? Workarounds might not be available for every flaw you—and a lot of other people—might find in the hard-wired Constitution. Sabato and Levinson are particularly exercised about the Senate's departure from the principle of representation in proportion to population, with the least pop-ulous states (currently Wyoming has the smallest population) having the same two votes that the largest states do. The Con-stitution says that we can't even amend the Constitution to change that. Article V, setting up the amendment procedure, says that "no State, without its Consent, shall be deprived of its equal Suffrage in the Senate." (Technically, we could amend the Constitution to give each state three or four or more senators, but that wouldn't solve the problem that concerns Sabato and Levinson.) I've played around trying to design workarounds for this problem, if it indeed is one. According to the Constitution, "Each House may determine the Rules of its Proceedings." Maybe the House could adopt a rule making it impossible without unanimous consent or a strong supermajority to adopt a proposal and send it to the president unless the proposal ʾined votes from senators representing states with a majority of the nation's population.[11] Would that deprive smaller states of their "equal Suffrage"?

Some provisions can't be worked around, though. We can't possibly work around constitutional provisions setting the number of years in the terms of our elected officials, limiting the number of terms a president can serve, and not limiting the number of terms our senators and representatives can serve.

Constitutional workarounds show that we can accomplish a lot if we have the political will—including placing effective term limits on senators and representatives by refusing to re-elect them. A lot, but not everything.

Changing the Hard-Wired Constitution: Process

Sabato and Levinson suggest that the best and perhaps only way to implement their suggestions is through a new constitutional convention. Their main concern is that legislators elected under current rules have few incentives to support their

11. This workaround would prevent the enactment of laws that didn't have the required support in the Senate, but it wouldn't directly address the difficulty of getting the Senate to approve legislation favored by senators from states with a majority of the nation's population. There might be some indirect effects, though, with senators from large states shaping their proposals to get just enough support from senators from smaller states.

proposed reforms. Sometimes it's because the legislators are the direct beneficiaries of those rules. Members of the House of Representatives elected from districts with boundaries drawn by partisan state legislatures aren't going to be enthusiastic about setting up a nonpartisan boundary-drawing commission. Sometimes it's because the reforms aren't urgent. Members of Congress could write a statute that addressed most of the issues raised by the possibility that a large number of elected government officials might be killed or disabled in a terrorist attack on Washington, but they haven't yet because the risk seems to be small and the political energy needed to enact such a statute, they believe, should be used on more urgent matters.[12]

Another reason for seeking a constitutional convention is—aha!—the Constitution's hard-wired amendment procedure. Article V, the Constitution's amendment provision, sets out several paths to constitutional amendment. The only one that's been used is proposal of an amendment by two-thirds votes in both houses of Congress, followed by ratification by three-quarters of the states, either in their legislatures or by special conventions.[13] These are quite stringent requirements. Mem-

12. Both Sabato and Levinson observe that statutory proposals have been introduced in Congress but have gone nowhere yet. Some of the difficulty arises from principled disagreement over statutory details.

13. The convention-based ratification procedure has been used only once, for the repeal of prohibition.

bers of Congress and state legislatures who benefit from the Constitution's hard-wired provisions are unlikely to support amending them unless there's overwhelming popular support. With substantial but not overwhelming popular support—a solid majority that on reasonable theories of democracy ought to be able to have its way—reform proposals will die as they slog through the usual amendment procedure.

Sabato and Levinson therefore suggest using the other Article V amendment process, which says that Congress "shall call a Convention for proposing Amendment" when the legislatures of two-thirds of the states apply for one. Legal scholars and politicians have raised interesting questions about this process: Must the applications from the states be identical? (Probably not, as long as they're reasonably consistent with each other.) Can Congress try to limit the subjects the constitutional convention will consider? (It can try, but the convention can probably lawfully propose amendments going beyond the limits Congress sets.) Those questions aside, we might wonder whether even the process of convening a constitutional convention can break the grip of political parties on constitution-making and amending. Legislatures controlled by those parties will organize the elections to the convention, set the campaign rules, and the like.

Perhaps an energized public would be able to break the grip of parties. It's certainly reasonable to think that any reform proposals that managed to get through a constitutional convention would carry political weight greater than each one might have as a statute or even as an individual constitutional amendment. And it might be reasonable to think that a popular mobilization for a constitutional convention would operate enough outside the parties that a convention would not be dominated by the parties.

Historically it's proven difficult to get the public mobilized behind "mere" good-government reforms such as those directed at the Constitution's hard-wired provisions. Major-party politicians have few incentives to make good-government reforms central to their platforms. They've reached their positions by using the processes already in place, and as a result are likely to think that those processes are good enough already. Ordinary citizens—the ones I've described as finding themselves regularly losing in ordinary political contention and in constitutional politics—typically care more about outcomes than about process. Someone has to persuasively send a complicated, several-stage message: "You're losing because the system is stacked against you. Instead of deploying your political energies to changing the outcomes you don't like, first deploy them to change the structure of politics, and then deploy them—or what political energy you still have left—to achieve the outcomes you want." A voter might reasonably think that it's more promising to go directly for the goal, the preferred policy outcomes.

Sometimes, though, good-government reforms actually do come about. The Progressive era in U.S. history—for our purposes, running from the late nineteenth century through the 1920s—saw significant changes in seemingly hard-wired rules: civil service and similar merit-based systems displacing patronage systems, direct election of senators displacing appointment by state legislatures, the spread of primaries to select party candidates for national office, and more. The mechanism of Progressive success is revealing. Good-government reformers organized as factions within existing parties and, when they failed to achieve success there, created third parties to put pressure on the major parties.[14] Eventually ambitious leaders within the major parties figured out that there was a pool of electoral support ready to be tapped. They proposed to insert some Progressive proposals in their party platforms, and this time they succeeded—because the reformers had demonstrated through their third-party efforts that they could deliver the votes.

If you think that the system is stacked against you, then you

14. What I've described is related to the description of how social movements affect constitutional politics, and perhaps good-government mobilizations should be called social movements as well. My sense, though, is that good-government movements are more closely tied to parties, including third parties, than the social movements discussed in Chapter Two.

can use ordinary politics either within the major parties or outside them to work around a good chunk of the hard-wired Constitution.

Conclusion

The political analysis I've outlined in this book is purely descriptive and, as I indicated in the introduction, pretty conventional among academics who study the Constitution. The descriptive account, though, might provide us with some ideas about how we—or perhaps better, you, the nonspecialist reader—should act. Seeing the Court and the Constitution in political terms democratizes them in an important way. Judges and lawyers have to worry about doctrine—three-part tests or specific rules, original understanding or living constitutionalism. Learning about doctrine takes time and effort, which most of us don't have.

Here the lessons of Senate confirmation hearings are valuable. Senators have their staffs prepare them to ask questions about a nominee's views on aspects of the Constitution that they and their constituents care about. Fair enough. The difficulty is that even with preparation for a high visibility performance, senators almost uniformly do a laughable job—from a specialist's point of view—describing the constitutional doctrines they are asking about. I don't fault them for that. They have a lot of other things on their minds—climate change legislation, reform of the health care system, the federal budget and its deficits. What the confirmation process shows, though, is that we shouldn't rely on our elected representatives—or ourselves—to get the Constitution "right" from a doctrinal or specialist point of view.

The political understanding of the Constitution I've offered here doesn't make strong demands on us, in terms of what we have to know about what the Supreme Court has said about the Constitution and why it matters in specific cases. The list of things you need to know—about the president, about the nature of the current constitutional regime, and the like—notably doesn't include anything about constitutional law as law. If you want the Constitution to matter in a different way, you don't have to go to law school so that you can argue cases before the Supreme Court.[15] All you have to do is be politically active. Look for a presidential candidate whose general vision about what the government ought to be doing is roughly similar to yours, and do whatever you would ordinarily do to support that

15. Although I do have to express my admiration for the commitment displayed by Michael Newdow, an eccentric physician and lawyer who unsuccessfully challenged the inclusion of the words "under God" in the Pledge of Allegiance—admiration not for the position he took, but for the fact that he insisted on arguing his own case when the Supreme Court heard it.

candidate—talk to your friends and neighbors, stand on street corners, contribute time or money to the candidate's campaign. And if you can't find a presidential candidate you like (or even if you can), find some civic association that is trying to mobilize support for something you care a lot about. In doing so you are being an exemplary constitutional citizen. To adapt a phrase from Charles Darwin, there is grandeur in this view of the Constitution.

sources

For a more detailed exposition of the general approach taken in this book, see Mark Tushnet, *The Constitution of the United States of America: A Contextual Analysis* (Oxford: Hart Publishing, 2009).

INTRODUCTION

Lincoln quotation: George S. Boutwell, *Reminiscences of Sixty Years in Public Affairs* (New York, McClure, Phillips and Co., 1902), vol. 2, p. 29.

Constitution outside the Constitution: Ernest A. Young, "The Constitution Outside the Constitution," 117 *Yale Law Journal* 408 (2007). There is a related literature on the Constitution outside the courts. For my contribution, see Mark Tushnet, *Taking the Constitution Away from the Courts* (Princeton: Princeton University Press, 1999).

Taken-for-granted features: A good discussion is H. Jefferson Powell, *A Community Built on Words: The Constitution in History and Politics* (Chicago: University of Chicago Press, 2002).

Most important issues: Harris Poll, Oct. 23, 2008, available at http://harrisinteractive.com/harris_poll/index.asp?PID=963; *BBC World News America,* The Harris Poll, Feb. 4, 2009, available at http://harrisinteractive.com/harris_poll/pubs/BBC_Harris_Poll_2009_02_04.pdf. For the most important examination of the theme developed in these paragraphs, see Frederick Schauer, "Foreword: The Court's Agenda—and the Nation's," 120 *Harvard Law Review* 4 (Oct. 2006).

Admissibility of hearsay: The reference is to *Boumediene v. Bush,* 553 U.S. (2008).

CHAPTER ONE. HOW THE
CONSTITUTION MATTERS

"Hard-wired" Constitution: An important recent work is Sanford Levinson, *Our Undemocratic Constitution: Where the Constitution Goes Wrong (And How We the People Can Correct It)* (New York: Oxford University Press, 2006). Related is Larry Sabato, *A More Perfect Constitution: 23 Proposals to Revitalize our Constitution and Make America a Fairer Country* (New York: Walker, 2007).

Political scientists and divided government: The basic work, details of which have been questioned, is David Mayhew, *Divided We Govern: Party Control, Lawmaking, and Investigations, 1946–2002,* 2d ed. (New Haven: Yale University Press, 2006).

Presidential administration: Elana Kagan, "Presidential Administration," 114 *Harvard Law Review* 2245 (2001).

Election of 1800: A good account of the constitutional dimensions of the 1800 presidential election is Bruce Ackerman, *The Failure of the Founding Fathers: Jefferson, Marshall, and the Rise of Presidential Democracy* (Cambridge: Harvard University Press, 2005).

Supreme Court and Guarantee Clause: *Luther v. Borden,* 48 U.S. (7 How.) 1 (1848).

New Deal/Great Society regime principles: For essays describing these principles, see Sidney M. Milkis and Jerome M. Mileur, eds., *The Great Society and the High Tide of Liberalism* (Amherst: University of Massachusetts Press, 2005).

Skowronek: Stephen Skowronek, *The Politics Presidents Make: Presidential Leadership from John Adams to Bill Clinton* (Cambridge, Mass.: Harvard University Press, 1993).

Actors, Athletes, and Astronauts: David T. Canon, *Actors, Athletes, and Astronauts: Political Amateurs in the United States Congress* (Chicago: University of Chicago Press, 1990).

"Too plain for argument": Quotation from *American Party of Texas v. White,* 415 U.S. 767 (1974).

Anderson case: *Anderson v. Celebrezze,* 460 U.S. 780 (1983).

Fusion decision: *Timmons v. Twin Cities New Party,* 520 U.S. 351 (1997).

Scalia quotation: *New York State Board of Elections v. Lopez Torres,* 552 U.S. 196 (2008).

Connecticut closed primary case: *Tashjian v. Republican Party of Connecticut,* 479 U.S. 208 (1986).

California blanket primary case: *California Democratic Party v. Jones,* 530 U.S. 567 (2000).

Burger on campaign finance: *Buckley v. Valeo,* 424 U.S. 1 (1976).

Campaign contribution limits: Taken from Campaign Finance Guide, http://www.campaignfinanceguide.org/guide-38.html.

Issue ad case: *Federal Election Comm'n v. Wisconsin Right to Life, Inc.,* 551 U.S. 449 (2007).

Express advocacy case: Citizens United v. Federal Election Comm'n, 130 S. Ct. (2010).

Millionaires' Amendment case: *Davis v. Federal Election Comm'n,* 554 U.S. (2008).

CHAPTER TWO. HOW THE SUPREME COURT MATTERS

Hamilton: *Federalist* 78.

Bickel: Bickel's argument, originally published in 1957, was elaborated in Alexander Bickel, *The Least Dangerous Branch: The Supreme Court at the Bar of Politics* (Indianapolis: Bobbs Merrill, 1962).

Powe: Lucas A. Powe, Jr., *The Warren Court and American Politics* (Cambridge, Mass.: Harvard University Press, 2002). Powe has more recently offered an overview of Supreme Court history pursuing the theme that the Court has always been more or less the instrument of then-governing elites. Lucas A. Powe, Jr., *The Supreme Court and the American Elite, 1789–2008* (Cambridge, Mass.: Harvard University Press, 2009).

Scholars on *Brown:* In addition to Powe, see Michael Klarman, *From Jim Crow to Civil Rights: The Supreme Court and the Struggle for Racial Equality* (New York: Oxford University Press, 2004), and Barry Friedman, *The Will of the People: How Public Opinion Has Influenced the Supreme Court and Shaped the Meaning of the Constitution* (New York: Farrar, Straus and Giroux, 2009).

Politics of Supreme Court nominations: A good source is David A. Yalof, *Pursuit of Justices: Presidential Politics and the Selection of Supreme Court Nominees* (Chicago: University of Chicago Press, 2001).

Brennan and sit-ins: For a description of the maneuvering, see

Michael Klarman, "An Interpretive History of Modern Equal Protection," 90 *Mich. L. Rev.* 213, 274–76 (1991).

Reagan Revolution and the Supreme Court: The argument sketched here is developed in more detail in Mark Tushnet, *A Court Divided: The Rehnquist Court and the Future of Constitutional Law* (New York: W. W. Norton, 2005).

Foisting issue off: The basic insight described here was first offered in Mark Graber, "The Nonmajoritarian Difficulty: Legislative Deference to the Judiciary," 7 *Studies in American Political Development* 35 (1993). It is developed in more detail in Keith Whittington, *Political Foundations of Judicial Supremacy: The Presidency, the Supreme Court, and Constitutional Leadership in U.S. History* (Princeton: Princeton University Press, 2007).

Hughes on low wages as subsidy: *West Coast Hotel Co. v. Parrish,* 300 U.S. 379 (1937).

Footnote Four: *United States v. Carolene Products Co.,* 304 U.S. 144 (1938).

"Constitution is color-blind": *Plessy v. Ferguson,* 163 U.S. 537 (1896).

Voluntary integration case: *Parents Involved in Community Schools v. Seattle Sch. Dist. No. 1,* 551 U.S. 701 (2007).

"Facetious": *Bowers v. Hardwick,* 478 U.S. 186 (1986). For an overview of the Supreme Court's treatment of gay rights claims, see Joyce Murdoch and Deb Price, *Courting Justice: Gay Men and Lesbian versus the Supreme Court* (New York: Basic, 2001).

Later gay rights cases: *Romer v. Evans,* 517 U.S. 620 (1996); *Lawrence v. Texas,* 539 U.S. 558 (2003).

Jeffries and Ryan: John C. Jeffries, Jr., and James Ryan, "A Political History of the Establishment Clause," 100 *Michigan Law Review* 279 (2001).

Reaffirming *Roe: Planned Parenthood of Southeastern Pa. v. Casey,*
505 U.S. 833 (1992), quotation from pages 866–67.

Sabato and Levinson: Larry Sabato, *A More Perfect Constitution: 23
Proposals to Revitalize Our Constitution and Make America a Fairer
Country* (New York: Walker, 2007); Sanford Levinson, *Our Undemocratic Constitution: Where the Constitution Goes Wrong (And How We
the People Can Correct It)* (New York: Oxford University Press, 2006).

Constitutional workarounds: For a more detailed discussion, see
Mark Tushnet, "Constitutional Workarounds," 87 *Texas Law Review*
1499 (2009).

Saxbe fix: For one discussion, see Michael Stokes Paulsen, "Is Lloyd
Bentsen Unconstitutional?", 46 *Stanford Law Review* 907 (1994).

Judicial term limits: For the proposal and some criticisms, see
Roger C. Cramton and Paul D. Carrington, eds., *Reforming the Court:
Term Limits for Supreme Court Justices* (Durham, N.C.: Carolina Aca-
demic Press, 2006).

acknowledgments

I thank my agent Sydelle Kramer for suggesting this project to me, and Michael O'Malley of Yale University Press for supporting it. Frank Michelman, L. Michael Seidman, and Adrian Vermeule made helpful comments on a draft and saved me from some embarrassing errors.

index

Abortion, 1–2, 128–29. *See also Roe v. Wade*

Adams, John, 29

Affirmative action, 137, 138

Anderson, John, 63–64

Article V amendment process, 168–69

Attack advertising, 90

Autonomy as a constitutional value, 147–48

Ballot access and the First Amendment, 63–65

Berlusconi, Silvio, 91

Bickel, Alexander, 95–96

Black, Hugo, 104

Blackmun, Harry, 114–15

Bork, Robert, 111

Bowers v. Hardwick, 142–43

Brennan, William J., 107, 114

Breyer, Stephen, 107

Brown v. Board of Education, 104, 105, 136–37

Brudney, Victor, 88

Bundling of campaign contributions, 82

Burger, Warren, 148

Bush, George H. W., 113

Bush, George W., 26–27, 123

Bush v. Gore, 105–6

Campaign finance regulation, 54, 74–91

Candidate recruitment, 50–56; and the First Amendment, 67–74

Cardozo, Benjamin, 113

Carter, Jimmy, 45–46

Christian Right, 148–49

Civil service system, 51

Clinton, Bill, 5, 24, 26, 46, 111

Closed primary elections, 69–72

Constitution, and fundamental rights, 11, 151–54; and political parties, 11–12; and creation of national government, 20–21; "hard-wired" provisions of, 22–23, 155–67; proposals to alter, 156, 167–70; "workarounds," 158–66

Constitution outside the Constitution, 6–8

Constitution Party, 64

Constitutional law, relation to politics of, 16–17; effects of social movements on, 139, 144–49

Constitutional "regimes," 41–45; life cycle of, 41–42, 49, 103, 118–26

Corporations and campaign finance, 86–88

Corruption and campaign finance regulation, 79–81

Countermajoritarian difficulty, 96

Court-packing proposal of 1937, 120–22

Divided government, 5–6, 24; general effects of, 24, 26; effects on judicial selection of, 111–12; effects on Supreme Court of, 123. *See also* Unified government

Dred Scott decision, 128, 129, 131

Duverger's Law, 37–38, 66–67

Eisenhower, Dwight, 107, 114

Electioneering communications, 86–87

Elections, constitutional provisions dealing with, 34–36

Electoral College, 28, 161–63

Emoluments Clause, 158–60

Equality as a constitutional value, 136–39

Federalism, implications for party structure of, 12–13, 25–26; and effects on party structure, 33–40; and relation to political parties, 49; and national constitutional rights, 99

Federalism Revolution of Rehnquist Court, 102–3

Federalist Papers, 95–96

Filibuster in Senate, 13–16, 21, 23

First Amendment, and political parties, 57–91; and two-party system, 65–67; and campaign finance, 74–91; and regulation of spending on campaigns, 75–77; and regulation to promote equality, 76–77; and regulation of contributions, 78–84; and regulation of independent expenditures, 84–88; and corporations, 86–88; and labor unions,

87–88; and legislators' self-interest, 88–89; and hydraulic theory of campaign finance, 91
Footnote Four, 135–36
Fund-raising, 55
Fusion candidates, 65–66

Gay and lesbian rights, 6, 140–42, 146–47
Gerrymandering, effects on party structure of, 31–32, 53–54, 55
Ginsburg, Ruth Bader, 6, 141
Green Party, 64
Griswold v. Connecticut, 98, 147–48
Guantanamo Bay, 10
Guarantee Clause, 34

Hamilton, Alexander, 95–96
Hoar, Ebenezer, 107–8
Hydraulic theory of campaign finance, 91

Impeachment, 46
Initiatives, 71, 88–89
Interest groups, effects on judicial selection of, 111–12
Issue advertising, 85–86

Jefferson, Thomas, 29
Johnson, Lyndon, 40, 101, 124–25

King Caucus, 50

Labor unions and campaign finance, 87–88
Lemon v. Kurtzman, 148
Levinson, Sanford, 155–56, 164–65, 167–70
Libertarian Party, 64
Lincoln, Abraham, 4–5, 129, 131

Marshall, Thurgood, 68–69
McCain-Feingold campaign finance act, 86
Mikva, Abner, 60
Millionaires' Amendment, 88–89

Nader, Ralph, 64
National power, growth of, 32–33
New Deal and Great Society constitutional regime, 42–43, 97, 101, 134–37
Newdow, Michael, 173
Nixon, Richard, 110, 114–15

Obama, Barack, 123–24
Open primary elections, 68
Outlier statutes, 98, 101–2, 104

Parker, John J., 111–12
Patronage appointments to Supreme Court, 107–8
Political parties, organization of, 13, 30–31; as coalitions, 15, 24–25, 30–31, 40, 49; as ideologically homogeneous, 15–16, 30–31; unmentioned in Constitution, 28; framers' views on, 28,

Political parties (*continued*)
30; membership in, 36–37; and
relation to local politics, 37; as
brand names, 39–40; con-
gressional and presidential, 48,
56; ideological homogeneity of,
50; conventions, 51; as ideologically homogeneous and effects
on judicial selection, 110–11; as
coalitions, and effects on Supreme Court, 110, 115, 127–28
Politics, and political parties, 11–12
Powe, L. A., 97–98, 99
Powell, Lewis F., 110, 141, 142–43, 144
Presidential administration, 26
Presidential election of 1800, 29–30
Presidential electors, 21. *See also*
Electoral College
Presidents, veto power of, 19, 23–
24; method of election, 28–29,
161–64; in party politics, 41–56;
reconstructive, 45, 46–47, 48–
49, 103; affiliated, 45; as party
leaders, 47–48; relation to Supreme Court of, 47; reconstructive, and conflicts with
Supreme Court, 118–23
Primary elections, 52; voting in,
53; and First Amendment, 59,
67–74; "open" and "closed,"
68–72; "blanket," 71–72;
"jungle," 72–73
Progressive Movement, 51–52, 171

Reagan, Ronald, 5, 44, 111, 122
Reagan Revolution, 41–43, 111,
137–39
Rehnquist, William H., 66, 143–44
Right to life, 1–2
Rights, disagreement about, 1–2,
152–54
Roberts, John, 86–87, 107
Roberts, Owen, 121
Roe v. Wade, 92, 93, 129, 131, 152–
53
Roosevelt, Franklin, 5, 116; at-
tempt to "purge" party, 56
Rutledge, Wiley, 108

Sabato, Larry, 155–57, 164–65,
167–70
Saxbe fix, 158–60
Scalia, Antonin, 71–72
Second Amendment, 2
Segregation, and effects on constitutional law of political parties,
60–61; effects on political parties of, 104
Senate, equal representation of
states in, 22, 166–67; method of
election of, 35; seniority system
in, 104–5; confirmation hearings in, 172–73
Separation of powers, 21–22; implications for party structure of,
12–13, 30–31
Seventeenth Amendment, 52

Sit-in cases, 117
Skowronek, Stephen, 45
Slavery, 127–28
Social movements and constitutional law, 6, 139, 144–49, 171
Social Security, 7
Sore-loser statutes, 64
Sotomayor, Sonia, 132
Souter, David, 114
Specter, Arlen, 14
State action doctrine, 60–61
Stone, Harlan Fiske, 135–36
Supreme Court, as rights-protector, 2–3; and issues of most concern to American people, 9–10; as serving politicians' interests, 96–106, 127–32; responsiveness to elite views, 105–6; responsiveness to ordinary politics, 117–18, 126; use to resolve or defer difficult political issues, 127–32
Supreme Court decisions, as affecting popular views about rights, 3
Supreme Court justices, as affected by politics, 4–5; considerations in appointing, 5; background, 104; role of politics in selection of, 106–18; role of regional and demographic representation in selection of, 108–9; role of ideology in selection of, 109–11; role of qualifications in selection of, 112–13; surprises after selection of, 113–14; constitutional visions of, 132–39; terms of, 164–66

Taft, William Howard, 120
Terry Schiavo law, 44–45
Thomas, Clarence, 113, 132
Twelfth Amendment, 32
Twenty-Second Amendment, 41
Two-party system and the Constitution, 65–67, 91

Unified government, 24, and Supreme Court, 95–106. *See also* Divided government

Van Buren, Martin, 50–51

Warren, Earl, 107, 113–14
Warren Court, 97–102, 109–10, 12–24
Women's rights, 6, 141–42, 146

Mark Tushnet is William Nelson Cromwell Professor of Law at Harvard University. A graduate of Yale Law School, he served as law clerk to Justice Thurgood Marshall and now specializes in constitutional law and theory, including comparative constitutional law. He lives in Washington, DC.